Top Shops!

A Beginner's Guide to Team Building and Shop Management

Top Shops!

A Beginner's Guide to Team Building and Shop Management

Robert G. Wilson
and
John D. Linscott

PUBLICATIONS

Hanser Gardner Publications
Cincinnati

Wilson, Robert G., 1942—

    Top Shops! : a beginner's guide to team building and shop management/Robert G. Wilson and John D. Linscott.

      p. cm.

    Includes bibliographical references.

    ISBN 1-56990-213-5 (alk. paper)

    1. Industrial management. 2. Organizational change. 3. Personnel management. 4. Work groups. 5. New business enterprises—Management. I. Linscott, John D. II. Title.

HD31.W5574 1996

658.4'02--dc20   96-9704

                                            CIP

Please direct all inquiries to:

    Hanser Gardner Publications
    6600 Clough Pike
    Cincinnati, OH 45244-4090
    800-950-8977

Printed in the United States of America.

1 2 3 4 5 6   01 00 99 98 97 96

Contents

Acknowledgements

We wish to acknowledge Mark D. Albert, Executive Editor of MODERN MACHINE SHOP, for encouraging us to produce this book. We also thank our tireless editor, Jennifer King, who made everything possible. She works beyond the expert level.

We would also like to thank our reviewers, Wayne S. Chaneski at the New Jersey Institute of Technology and Dr. Joel D. Wisner at the University of Nevada at Las Vegas College of Business and Economics, for their recommendations and support.

We dedicate this book to our fathers—both machinists—Chester G. Wilson and Clarence O. Linscott.

Preface

Ben is a retired machinist. He is friendly, soft-spoken, and pleased to have someone listen to his stories. He made certain our coffee cups were full and kept pushing a box of fresh donuts in our direction as he talked.

One of Ben's first jobs, after he dropped out of college, was removing slag from the seams of fresh welds in fuel tanks and in ships' hulls. Dangerous work. Fuel fumes still resided in some of the tanks and Ben saw more than one explosion. He eventually attended trade school at night to become a machinist. After graduating from trade school, he took a job as a machine operator in a shop that manufactured aircraft parts. He worked hard and eventually was doing his own CNC programming and setups. One day Ben said to himself, "If this company can make money operating in this way, then so can I."

Ben eventually bought an old engine lathe and a small mill a friend had been storing in his shop. He cleaned them up and got them working. A welder he knew who worked for a lumber mill introduced him to the mill's owner, who gave Ben his first contract as a machinist.

Over the years Ben either worked in shops or owned his own shop. He has run into many problems that face a shop owner. But he can also see things from the other side. As a machinist, he knows many of the problems a machinist has with a shop owner.

When asked why he had owned his own shop several times, but always sold it and went back to work as a machinist for someone else, Ben responded, "It was too much work. I worked around the clock. Besides, I could never grow beyond five or six people."

Many people, like Ben, struggle with the business of running a job shop. A machine shop is unique, and the struggle—and the victory—can be charted on a clock.

- **One o'clock**—you sense discontentment; something seems wrong. Jobs aren't going through the shop as smoothly as they could be.
- **Two o'clock**—you feel things may be okay, but they may get worse, and you start to worry. Late deliveries are beginning to take their toll on the customers and your work load.
- **Three o'clock**—you feel things are sliding. You have to hurry. You hire more people to get the jobs through.
- **Four o'clock**—you jump in. It's imperative that you turn things around.
- **Five o'clock**—you wonder who you are and where you are going. Scrap is killing you and the schedule is getting worse.
- **Six o'clock**—you buy *Top Shops!* and start reading. Your first step is to clarify your vision, mission, strategy, and goal.
- **Seven o'clock**—you know who is important to you in your business.
- **Eight o'clock**—you define your areas of success from the viewpoints of those relationships that are important to you.
- **Nine o'clock**—you describe goal areas essential to your success.
- **Ten o'clock**—you set numerical levels for each goal.
- **Eleven o'clock**—you form unique natural teams to carry out goals.
- **Twelve o'clock**—you reward the winners!

This is what *Top Shops!* is all about. We have included only essential information. The topics in each chapter are kept short because each contains the heart of the necessary information you need. We wrote the book so the shop owner or manager and his key employees would have a road map to get them from where they are now to the next corner and beyond. Of course, you don't do this alone. Everyone in your shop does it with you, all the while increasing production to keep profits up.

If you're a shop owner or manager, *Top Shops!* will help you grow beyond five or six employees. *Top Shops!* shows you how to take days or weeks off without worry, regardless of how many employees you have. Those who work for you need *Top Shops!* so they know how to run your business whether you're there or not. They need it so they can share your vision of creating a top shop.

Today we are confronted by many new horizons: intellectual, social, and technological. People have new and often challenging expectations of each other. Things are not the way they used to be. The good old days are gone, yet the enterprising machine shop owner knows the field is wide open.

There are many books on management and organizational change. Yet in the final outcome, when all is said and done, lots more is said than done. *Top Shops!* is a book of action. You can actually do what the book suggests. *Top Shops!* shows you how to manage people with creativity and form a team environment so your shop can succeed in the machining business.

Robert G. Wilson
John D. Linscott
Seattle, June 1996

Chapter 1
Getting on Track

▪ Your Place at the Top

As the top person in a machine shop, you have creativity, intelligence, and talent, otherwise you wouldn't be where you are. To use an example, think about the boardroom table in a large corporation. Those who sit around a boardroom table are people with proven ability, otherwise they could not possibly be where they are. Top people are treated with respect and their ideas are listened to. Most likely, they have moved up through the company through years of dedicated service, and they have some degree of job security.

These top executives have certain qualities in common. They enjoy their jobs, cherish the company, enhance the workplace, and care about others. They often start work early and frequently work more than a forty-hour work-week.

What do you have in common with corporate executives? You have put in the same number of hours as they have, maybe more. You've come up through the ranks like many of them. You cherish your company, want to enhance your workplace, and care about the employees in your shop. You want your employees to do their best, because not only are they doing something for themselves, they are also helping put your company on top.

Whether you inherited the business, bought it, or started it from scratch, or whether you are managing your shop for an off-site owner, you are just like those top-level corporate executives. As the top person, you must focus your energy and resources on one thing: where your business is going next.

It is the machine shop manager who propels his company into the future. No one else can do this. The decisions you make to take your company into the future—to meet the demands and challenges ahead—depend mostly on two things. First, your ability to make creative decisions. And second, your ability to effectively manage others to successfully do their jobs, so you have the freedom to develop and implement your long-range plans.

■ In the Beginning

If you started your own machine shop, you probably did so because you wanted to have a good job. You believed you could create a unique business and run it better than anyone else. You didn't want anyone telling you what to do. You wanted to be the boss rather than be bossed. At some time you may even have said to yourself, "Why should I work for $9.25 an hour for someone else when I can do this work myself and charge my customers $45.00 an hour?"

Let's take a look at what sometimes happens when you take the big step of starting your own machine shop. Let's say you quit your job. You invest in a Bridgeport mill or perhaps a small CNC mill, a lathe, a saw, and a variety of other support equipment. You contact potential customers who offload machined parts. You get some invoices and envelopes printed and obtain a business license. You convince your spouse to answer the phone while you crank the handles.

Most likely you performed nearly all of the tasks in the beginning. You were closely involved in selling, calling on customers, running your office, chasing down tools and materials, and machining parts at night when the phones were not ringing. You may also have had responsibility for all bookkeeping, often doing it at home after hours. As demand for your machining services increased, it became necessary to hire people to perform each of the functions you used to perform. The success of your business then became dependent upon your ability to effectively manage the people involved—people doing the jobs you once did.

Or perhaps your story is slightly different. Perhaps you started out at an entry-level job, and have worked your way up to top-level manager. But whether you came in at the top or worked your way up, it makes no difference to where you are now. If you have successfully guided your shop to the level of growth in which you need additional employees, you should be congratulated.

But have you accomplished all you set out to achieve? Do you feel like you're working too many hours without arriving at your destination? Are you happy with your business as it is, or do you think you could do more? Are you confident of future success, or are you concerned about losing jobs to your competitors?

Many managers find themselves frustrated by the problems of day-to-day operations and worried over the future of their shops. You may have become trapped in spending all your time on troubleshooting, and have little or no time left for planning for the larger issues. Even if you can find time to study the big picture and try new approaches to meet coming challenges, you may not know what steps to take. How do you get back on track?

■ Getting Past the Problems to Solutions

In general, it's not one thing that gets a business off track, but a series of events, a combination of decisions often made in good faith, the ups and downs of the economy, and seemingly unimportant issues that have evolved into major problems. But it's important not to dwell on the reasons a business begins to have problems. What's important is to focus on solutions.

To solve the big problems, ask yourself:

1. What steps should I take to get my business back on track?
2. What skills do I need to propel my company into the future?

The Most Common Problems a Machine Shop Faces

Disequilibrium—Disequilibrium occurs when a shop is out of whack, and nothing seems to be going right. Different departments (production, accounting, sales, estimating, planning, manufacturing) blame each other for all the company's woes. Material is not purchased on time, or not enough material is

(cont.)

◼ The Most Common Problems... *(continued)*

purchased. The tooling isn't right. The CNC program doesn't make good parts. The job was underbid. There's lots of grumbling and finger pointing. What the company needs is a plan to pull things together to get everyone going in the same direction.

Outdated Technology—New technology is needed when there is a major shift in development, or possibly when you are anticipating a major new contract. Perhaps you must get new equipment in order to meet the new productivity and pricing requirements of a customer. Perhaps you need to develop new ways of doing things to meet your new challenges. Of course, new equipment usually means additional training, too.

Moving Away from the Base—A shop may move away from its original base when the company is doing work it never intended to do. As an example, if your base of service is to provide general machining services to aircraft manufacturers, and your equipment consists basically of manual lathes and mills, you probably don't want to take on long bed stretch-formed parts. If you are not familiar with the procedures required to manufacture high heat-treat parts, or you aren't certified to make such parts, you should probably stay away from them as well. If you've been forced—whether through poor decisions, good decisions, or just the nature of things—into areas you're unfamiliar with, you need help focusing on how to handle new developments.

Weakened Social Conditions—Many machine shops need to improve the social aspect of the work environment. Some signs of poor social conditions are finding people consistently late for work, the existence of competition instead of cooperation among departments and individuals, and sloppy workmanship or high scrap rates. Poor social conditions usually develop when management is concerned with results to the point of ignoring employee needs. These poor attitudes usually result in a high turnover rate, a "revolving-door" of employment.

Changing Hands—When a business changes hands—for example, when the company has just been sold or is taken over by another family member—it may be time to do a complete analysis of the business in order to obtain insights into making the transition smoothly or increasing productivity. This may also

(cont.)

■ The Most Common Problems... *(continued)*

be the time to break old habits and focus on increased performance. New owners with little or no experience in job shop operation can ultimately bring the company to its knees if they do not catch on quickly. Even if the new owners have previous manufacturing experience, a machine shop will fail if they don't have a clear understanding about what a shop is and how it works.

The natural condition of a business is to grow. If it doesn't grow, it dies. And the reason most businesses don't grow is because the top people don't know how to make them grow.

The real difference between success or failure in any machine shop is how well those in charge bring out the creative talents of their people. When we look at an organization that has lasted through the years, we see that it does not owe its continued existence to good administrative skills—as important as these are—but to the devotion and talents of its people who have had an active part in building it. The employees who have held the company together through lean times and good times have brought the company to where it is today.

■ The Making of a Legend

In every company's past, certain individuals stand out as heroes. Although many of these heroes were top-level people, not all of them were. A hero might be the planner, a machinist, or even a shipping clerk. Whatever such people did, and whoever they were, they left their mark on the company. "Old timers" speak of them with respect, recalling their contributions.

What was their contribution? Why and how did they contribute more than the average employee? If you were to ask a legend to sit down and tell you how he became a legend, what would that person say?

Most likely the "legend" would tell you that the company encouraged him to contribute something of himself. His supervisors didn't stand in his way. Because of this, the legendary person was patient during difficult times, understanding during belt-tightening times, and enthusiastic during periods of

(cont.)

The Making of a Legend...(continued)

growth. His job was more than a paycheck. It was a way he could express himself and see the work he did take shape. Invariably the legend did this because someone up the line—the owner, manager, or supervisor—listened to him and took his ideas seriously.

You can dramatically slow or stop the growth of your business if you don't know how to manage people. For example, you may be an excellent machinist—that's why you got into the business in the first place. But for your business to grow in size and volume you must hire people and work with people. Working with people is very different than cranking handles or programming CNC equipment. Most machine shop owners have never had a course in management—and why should they? They are experts at what they do best: machining parts.

As the top person of a successful machine shop you must manage people, not machines. Your employees set up and run the machines. If you want to keep your best people—and it's the best people who will really make your business work—it's important that you first learn what your job is. Then it's important to learn basic ways of getting your people to do what you want done, even when you're not there.

■ Recognizing "Top Shops"

Before you can learn to manage people effectively and propel your company into the future, you must first understand what a "top shop" looks like. Following are top shop characteristics. No shop necessarily displays all these qualities, and many of these qualities take time to develop. However, the ideal top shop:

- Fulfills your vision. Your shop is in the process of becoming what you originally conceived it to be. Your mind controls your shop.
- Follows your ideas. Shop employees look to you for leadership.
- Responds positively to local economic challenges. Your shop is able to diversify when necessary and adapts when required.

- Is clean, neat, and environmentally safe. By definition, a shop is not the neatest place to work. However, paying attention to health codes and safety requirements, providing proper waste disposal, having uncluttered aisles and the like makes the shop a visibly attractive place to work and shows customers and employees these characteristics are important to you.
- Evokes a sense cooperation. You can walk into some shops and immediately "feel" a sense of cooperation between different departments, such as office personnel, sales, and machinists, as well as among those working on the same job.
- Provides a "team atmosphere" within the shop by organizing employees into teams, and encouraging teamwork with clients and with neighbors.
- Supports its professionals. A top shop identifies professionals early and nurtures them through compensation, rewards, and job security. Strong shops are supported on the shoulders of experts.
- Focuses on growth. A top shop is not afraid to grow. In fact, a top shop looks forward to growth! Growth is welcome because the shop manager has his teams in place and they are trained to handle growth.
- Is driven by customers. A top shop responds to customer needs of timeliness, scheduling, and quality.
- Has the latest accounting system that keeps track of all costs and revenues so you know where you are at every moment.
- Uses the latest technology.
- Actively participates in neighborhood and civic events, and is a member of one or more professional groups.
- Sets goals and works toward them.

In the following chapters, we will explore the steps you, the top person, need to take to create a top shop:

1. Understand your role as the shop's leader, and develop your corporate vision, mission, strategy, and goals.
2. Prepare to handle all reactions to change, both negative and positive.
3. Help each person focus on his unique role by providing the support your employees deserve.

4. Identify the critical relationships for all shop employees.
5. Help your employees succeed by determining how to meet others' expectations.
6. Set numerical goals based on success areas.
7. Identify poor performance and star performance among your amateurs, nonprofessionals, professionals, and experts. Keep the amateurs moving toward the expert level, and keep your experts on top.
8. Motivate people at the right times and in the right places by reinforcing good behavior, discouraging negative behavior, and ignoring what is unimportant.
9. Offer tangible and nontangible rewards to get the behavior that leads to the results you want.
10. Move your shop into a team environment, and unleash your employees' potential.

These steps are positive, specific, and bring immediate and long-range results. After these steps have been taken, and the change process is under way, people know what is expected of them and they can sense where the business is going. Your demonstrated leadership skills will take your shop straight to the top!

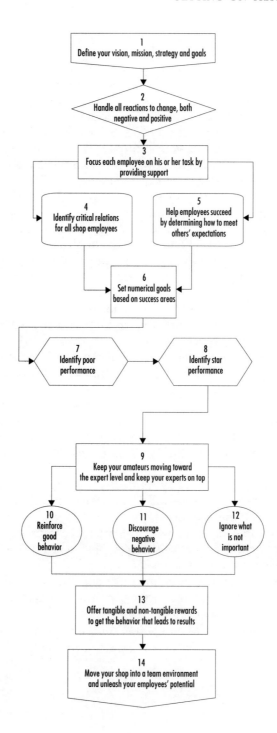

Ten Quick Tips to Putting Your Business on Top

1. Have a picture in your mind of where you want your business to go. What's your definition of a "top shop"? If you don't have a clear, concrete goal, you won't ever get there.
2. Always think one customer ahead. Identify the specific type or types of services you wish to provide to your customers. For example, is it your plan to specialize in long bed milling or perhaps Blanchard grinding or turning? Or is it your desire to provide general machining services? Ask yourself if your current equipment list can support the type of services you plan to provide.
3. Things change, and you must learn to accept that. You have no control over changes that come your way unless you are prepared to meet them with a positive outlook.
4. Create a business that works without you, that keeps going when you're not in the shop. Work *on* your business, not *in* your business. A good way to begin is to write down an organizational chart starting with yourself. Organize the business by functions, not by people.
5. People development is an essential goal because you can't make people do anything. You can only create an environment that makes people want to perform at their best.
6. Set the example. A boss tells people what to do, but a leader sets the example. Setting the example doesn't mean you have to do the work better or faster than anyone else. It simply means that you demonstrate integrity and commitment.
7. Develop your "soft system." It is the way you treat others and the tone and tempo of the words you use in your business communications.
8. Develop your "hard system"—the tools, training, and equipment you use to make your people the best so they can give your customers A-1 products.
9. Think big. Remember, the difference between big business and small business is that a big business is a small business that did all the right things.
10. Be patient. Good things don't happen all at once.

Chapter 2
The Top Person

■ Your Unique Function

Everyone in a business must have a necessary function, something he does that either brings in money or saves the company money. The higher up you go in the shop, the more difficult it is to identify what each person does that no one else does. Yet everyone must have a unique function, otherwise what are they being paid for?

As a machine shop manager, think about your unique function. Ask yourself these questions:

1. What do I do that no one else does?
2. If I were suddenly gone, what void would be left in the company?
3. How hard would it be to fill that void?

The answers to these questions help define what you do that no one else does.

What the top person does that no one else can do is provide the leadership and guidance needed to keep the company moving in the intended direction, and to provide the energy and motivation required to keep everyone productive. The top person is also the company's eyes into the future. Everyone sees the future differently, but the top person sees where he wants his company to go, and takes it in that direction. If there is no top person—or visionary—in the company, there can never be agreement on which direction the company can or should go, and the company does not go anywhere.

If the top person were suddenly gone, the company would flounder. Who would be there to hold things together? Who would give the company focus and direction? At first employees might show up for work and perform their assigned tasks, as they do daily. They might work several days—or weeks—without feeling the impact of no owner present. But eventually they would realize there is no one to make the vital decisions that plan, organize, lead, and control the outcome. The company would soon begin to disintegrate.

It would be difficult to fill a void left by a top person. Not everyone, no matter how skillful, has the capacity or ability to lead a company. A top person must make long-range and short-range plans, effectively and skillfully organize his experts and top people, clearly convey his vision, and establish those controls that keep the company focused.

■ Qualities for Success

Ask yourself why you started your machine shop, or why you chose to accept the top position. In most cases, taking the lead begins with an impulse. Perhaps you simply got tired of running other people's machines. You saw a better way to make parts, had an idea about how to do it, and followed through. This is not an easy task.

It takes three key qualities to start a business, and to make the business a success: intelligence, creativity, and follow-through. Each of these keys are represented as a circle, as shown in the accompanying diagram. Not everyone possesses these three key elements in equal proportion. Each person has a greater or lesser degree of each. We all know people who are very intelligent, yet seem to lack creativity. Some individuals are very creative, yet appear to be unable to follow through on their ideas. And some individuals are intelligent and have good follow through, but their efforts lack the pizzazz, the creativity, that could easily put them over the top.

Success at running your machine shop cannot be attained unless these three qualities are present, as shown in the following diagram where I = Intelligence, C = Creativity, and F = Follow-through.

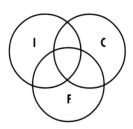

Your potential for success can be measured by how well you integrate these three key characteristics. The portion in the diagram that shows where the three circles intersect demonstrates the potential for success. The more these characteristics overlap, the greater your "focus," or possibility for success. *Focus* is a word commonly used, and often overused, in business. Being focused means integrating your intelligence, creativity, and follow-through to achieve your goals.

One trait successful, creative people have in common is that they don't allow anything to divert them from their course. A CEO of a top corporation once said, "I don't have enough managers with one-track minds." What he meant, of course, was that not enough managers in his corporation were focused on results—getting the job done. Most were involved in unimportant, therefore unnecessary and unproductive, activities. Successful people, on the other hand, stick to their main objective by wisely using their intelligence, creativity, and follow-through.

Reflect on how you manifest these three key qualities. Which ones are your strong points, and which ones are your weakest? Usually you will be strong in two of these characteristics, and will need to strengthen the one in which you are weakest.

If you easily recognize the area in which you are weakest, don't worry about it too much. There are no specific rules of guidance that can change a weak key characteristic into a stronger one, save a personal commitment to work at it. However, consider the following:

1. Move from strength to strength. Don't overly concern yourself with your one key characteristic of weakness. Instead, work to continually develop your strong areas while at the same time keeping in mind your weakest characteristic. Developing your strong areas never makes up for the one area you are weakest in, but it gives you greater confidence. This increases your leadership skills.

2. Respect those individuals in your employ, or others you know such as personal friends or your spouse, who possess the key characteristic you seem to lack. People are often attracted to those who share similar characteristics and possess, in abundance, the one characteristic you lack but admire. Watch how those you admire operate, and how they use their skills in that area you are weakest in. Learn from them.

3. "When you buy a dog, you don't have to learn to bark." Hire individuals who demonstrate characteristics in the one area you are weakest in, and rely on them to provide strength in that area. This is also the main benefit of teamwork: it brings together people with complementary strengths.

In general, develop yourself through reading, study, and listening to others. Take risks. Personal growth, just like growth in business, is achieved by taking a certain amount of risks, by trying new things. Sometimes you will want to do things the competition does, only because it works. But there are times you will want to try something new and leave the competition behind.

Occasionally go outside your sphere of interests to pick up new ideas. This helps crystallize your vision. Attend a lecture, go to a concert, visit an art gallery, take up a new hobby or a new sport, or join a professional group.

■ The Top Person's First Four Steps

Every company has a top official: a Chief Executive Officer (CEO), president, owner, or manager. This top person, whether chairman of the board of a large corporation or the owner of a two-person business, has four unique responsibilities. This individual is unique because no one in the organization has as much influence over the following concerns, or can deal with them as effectively, as the top person.

1. Vision—where the company is going
2. Mission—what the company stands for
3. Strategy—how the company will get there
4. Goals—how the company is doing along the way

The Vision

Your vision is your company's future state, the foundation upon which the strategy for moving forward is built. As the top person, it is your unique responsibility to envision the company's future and steer it in that direction. Remember, your vision is also the idea that got your company going. It's the motivation that started the business. Those who work at peak performance move the company toward the vision.

CASE STUDY   Semaphore Manufacturing is a small shop in the industrial section of a large midwestern city. David Kroznowski is the owner, and his customers are primarily nearby electronics firms, for which he manufactures custom panels.

David's father started Semaphore during World War II, manufacturing metal cases for portable field radios used by the U.S. Army. David hopes to eventually move the business more into general electronics, although he still maintains several government contracts.

David's father's original vision was to own a shop employing about 15 to 20 machinists. He wanted his shop to provide himself and his employees with a greater income than could be made elsewhere. Also, he wanted a business that would support him when he retired.

David's father also wanted to employ family members so they could carry on the business, and David has taken over the business. His vision today includes plans to move his company's location to a new industrial park, and to go after contracts with computer companies to manufacture computer cases.

To do this, he knows it is important to maintain—even exceed—his present level of production. This will give him the capital, as well as the encouragement, to go after new contracts, even as his father did fifty years earlier.

To understand the vision, consider the intent of your company in the broadest philosophical sense. Ask yourself, "How clear am I on where this company should be going?" In other words, if there isn't a clear vision, get one! If you've lost sight of your vision, recover it! Is your company still powered by its original vision, or has the vision changed? A vision should not change, at least not very much.

To re-connect with your vision of your company, think about the spark that first made you want to operate your own machine shop. If you have been in business awhile, or have purchased or inherited the business, try to re-experience the original impulse that started the business. What caused the impulse? Did someone come up with one good idea? Did *you* come up with a good idea? Ask yourself, "What is the motivation behind my company, the idea that got my company going?"

Whether you're the original founder or not, it is possible for you to identify with the roots of the company—what the company's founder had in mind when the shop was started. When you do so, you quickly become part of the company. And the same is true for your employees. When they begin to identify with what the company is all about and why it exists, they become part of its onward course into the future.

To help everyone focus on the company's vision, you, as top person, must enkindle excitement about the future. Share the vision in such a way that those who work with you value the company's future and want to become part of it. After all, their jobs and their future with the company are inseparable from the direction the company is going. To achieve this united participation in the future, the emphasis must be on working together to turn your vision into reality.

The best way to share your vision with others may be to meet with your key people and explain your vision to them. Invite their response. Tell them to use their own discretion in sharing this information with those whom they supervise. This accomplishes several important things. First, by giving your department heads or team leaders "inside" information and bringing them into your confidence, you are demonstrating respect for them and thereby establishing tacit support for your ideas. Second, by putting them in charge of disseminating your vision to their subordinates, you support their position in the company.

It's important that when you share your vision with others in your company, you do not make promises. What you are sharing is an abstraction, a glimpse of the "promised land." As tempting as it is, don't talk about personal details regarding salary increases, promotions, or additional benefits. Discuss only how you see the company in years ahead, what you will be doing, what the facility will be like, what types of new contracts you will be working on, and how you will be organized.

Regard your company's present condition as one step on a long road to realizing that dream. Everything being done now should move the company toward your renewed vision. You can realize the company's vision through singleness of purpose, identifying strategies, and setting goals.

For Owners:
Putting a Dollar Value on Your Machine Shop

As long as you are in the process of establishing, or re-establishing, your vision for your company, you may want to think about what you hope to get out of the business when you decide to move on.

Equity is the sole purpose for building a business. Your shop consists only of your equity and reputation, nothing else. Fortunately, equity and reputation are controlled by your mind—by your ability to use your intelligence, creativity, and follow-through to establish your vision, mission, strategy, and goals. Only you can take steps to increase the value of your business.

There are three ways to value a business: income, profit, and equity. *Income* is all money coming in, or cash flow. Every business needs cash to continue operating. But income is not as important as profit. *Profit* is what is left over after all payroll and bills are paid. If you don't make a profit, something's wrong. You're working too hard for too little, or you're spending too much money. But the most important of all is *equity*, what your shop is worth. It is the value of your machinery, equipment, and all things under your control. It is also your reputation—what customers think when they hear your shop's name.

Build your shop as though you want to sell it at any moment, even if you never have any intention of selling it. Clean up your shop, sweep up the chips, and keep the oil off the floor. Clean

(cont.)

> **For Owners:...**(continued)
> and maintain the machines and keep the tool room in order.
> Make sure each work station is clean. Then take the necessary
> steps to building a healthy reputation.
>   A business must produce a predictable result every time.
> The true value of a business is that it produces predictable
> results which are achieved as the business builds equity.

The Mission

The mission is your company's purpose, its job, its particular task. It is what your company hopes to accomplish, today and in the future. Mission differs from vision in that the vision is insubstantial, the dynamics behind motivation. The mission is your company's practical, overall goal. The mission is usually what your company does either better than, faster than, or more uniquely than any other company of its type.

Here's an example: A company originally designed and manufactured brakes for locomotives. Today, that same company builds shuttle equipment for NASA. Although the products and services have changed, the original mission is the same—to produce equipment that makes transportation better, safer, and faster.

It doesn't matter if your company's original product has changed over the years, or if your company has diversified by striking out in new and interesting directions. What's important is to lock in on what your mission has been, or more importantly, what it should be. Use it to carry your shop into the future and meet obstacles as they arise.

To help identify your company's mission, consider this: what does your shop deliver that would make a customer call you and no one else? Do you offer exceptional quality, a fair price, and on-time delivery? Does the customer trust your company to deliver what was promised? Does your customer have confidence in your products and services?

The mission contains information that shapes and drives the company. It provides direction for corporate goals, and defines the company's culture. In general, a customer selects your company to do business with because you possess one or more of these important qualities: excellent work, low cost, or quick service. Thus, a good way to sum up your company's mission is to have a slogan. The slogan should say something about your greatest strength, whether it be quality, service, expertise, or price. Consider these popular slogans, noting that each slogan emphasizes either price, speed, or quality:

Leadership Through Service
Quality You Can Expect
Merchandise Priced Right
I Love What You Do For Me
We Try Harder
Radio Dispatched Service
You Have the Problem? We Find the Answer

CASE STUDY   Laura Pendleton is CEO of Avalon Machine Works. She had years of experience in manufacturing her product, and eventually helped her shop grow from one assistant to two full-time salesmen, five machinists, and a small assembly line. Most of her work came through electronics firms.

Laura frequently found herself trying to resolve arguments between her two salespeople. There seemed to be a great deal of confusion and disagreement about Avalon's purpose. Things got so bad at times that sides were taken even among shop personnel, and the resulting consequences affected production.

Laura took two steps that finally solved the problems and brought an end to the arguments.

First, she formed a board of directors, a group of advisors she trusted. The members of the board consisted of herself, the shop foreman, her senior salesman, and a local university professor whom she knew.

She announced to her employees that the company now had a board of directors that would take up certain management issues. This announcement alone seemed to diffuse some of the uneasiness.

Then, she scheduled the first meeting of the board for 10:00 a.m. on a Wednesday in the small lunchroom next to her office. There was one topic on the agenda: select a company slogan.

Laura later commented that this was the best meeting she had ever attended. The process of selecting a company slogan

(cont.)

forced everyone on the board to focus on what the company was all about. Did the company want to offer quick and timely service, even if it meant dropping everything to rush an order through, as one salesman insisted that it should? Or, did it want to produce quality parts and establish a reputation of excellence? Were they specializing in a certain type of work, like milling or turning, or did the company want to provide general machining services?

The process of thinking through what the company was all about produced a list of assets such as experience, quality, care, attention to detail, etc. After several hours of exciting deliberation, the slogan Laura and her board came up with was:

Experience You Can Trust

The board concluded these qualities, or attributes, would best be expressed in this slogan.

To get this message across to her employees, Laura asked everyone in the company to attend a meeting, first thing, on a Friday morning. Laura served donuts and coffee.

Present at the meeting were the members of her board of directors, whom she introduced. She had asked one of the board members—the university professor who was not directly associated with her company, and who was the least known—to introduce the new slogan which expressed the company's new direction. He did this by giving everyone a coffee mug imprinted with the new Avalon logo, and the slogan, "Experience You Can Trust."

Laura explained that the new-found purpose of Avalon Machine Works was a new commitment to machining quality parts with on-time deliveries. She explained that one without the other was of little or no value to the customer. Laura emphasized that producing quality parts on time takes a great deal of team effort, and that Avalon Machine Works has the experience and expertise to provide this service.

Later she met with her two salesmen privately and asked them to bring any problems to her.

From that point forward the bickering about how fast an order should be filled, whether or not the customer was getting the right price for the job, and so on, became incidental. The overriding principle as expressed in the company's slogan emphasized to the customer and employees alike that experience and quality were the heart of Avalon Machine Works.

The Strategy

Your strategy is your "big picture" plan for moving forward toward your vision, and for fulfilling your mission. Your role as the top person is to make sure everyone moves in the same direction.

A well-conceived strategy, or business plan, accommodates trends and unforeseen developments. Developments frequently arise that upset the game plan, but this does not alter the strategy. A good business plan turns a crisis into an opportunity.

A good strategy consists of:

1. The specific services you provide your customers. Is yours a long bed milling shop? Is it a grinding shop? Do you provide general machining services? Consider the investment required for each type of service.
2. A general idea or statement summing up how the shop is doing. This includes the ability to forecast, observe trends, and stay on top of things. Ask yourself, what is the competition doing? From the customer's viewpoint, how do we rate against our competitors? Are we still a name player in the market?
3. An idea of where you're going. What happens next? Should you shift gears? Are you competitive with other firms in your market? Do events require you to alter some plans?
4. An idea of how to get to your goals. What is required for your company to take the next step? Are you ready? What needs to be done to put you over the top?
5. The necessary personnel, time, money, and equipment to make it happen. Are your people ready? Do they have the support they need? Are they trained? Does each person get the vital information needed to make important decisions?

These are not simple questions to answer. Nor should you attempt to answer them once and remain fixed on those answers forever. You may want to re-evaluate your answers periodically, letting your strategic viewpoint evolve over time. Consider these questions as topics to talk over with others, and hold special meetings to discuss them.

Goals

Goals are indicators that allow you to measure the shop's progress as you go along. Think in terms of big goals, visionary goals, not the specific goals of daily operation.

Goals lead to the future, and it's up to the top person to prepare for the future. A supervisor is mostly concerned with the day-to-day operations of his department. A foreman concentrates on specific jobs. But the top person's goal for his business is the big picture. These goals don't need to be written, or even be observable. Your intuitive sense can tell you when the big goals have been reached. You know something great has been accomplished.

As with strategies, you should involve your employees in establishing goals for the company. The more direct information you have, the better you can prepare for your company's future. Some of the possible goal areas for which you might want to consult your employees include:

1. Improvement of products or services
2. Implementation of new technologies
3. Reduction of costs
4. Product development or expansion into new services

By asking your employees to keep you up-to-date on what's going on, you create an atmosphere of open communication in which they will want to tell you everything. When you receive the information you need to drive your business forward, use it to set goals and develop and fine-tune your operations.

When one of these large goals, or milestones, is attained, recognize the achievements and reward your company. For example, attaining a goal might result in installing CAD software, purchasing certain machinery, hiring an additional worker, or initiating a tool management system.

■ The Board of Directors: Your Guidance Team

When most businessmen think about a board of directors, they think in terms of large corporations, smoke-filled boardrooms, and people speaking in hushed whispers. Large corporations have a board of directors for one main reason: to help keep the company on track.

Though a board of directors is vital to a large organization, it is also of great benefit to a small operation. Even if you only have a few employees, a small board of directors—perhaps three or four people—can be a valuable asset. A board can assist you in setting strategic goals, help you view events from different perspectives, suggest company policy, and offer ideas for expansion and growth. The board can advise you on what steps to take and how best to achieve these goals.

In general, a board of directors meets once every few months, maybe once each business quarter. The board looks over your profit and loss statement with you, as well as your forthcoming business decisions, such as hiring additional employees, purchasing additional tools or equipment, and extending your employees' hours.

The value of a board of directors is to give you insights and help chart the future of your company in ways you did not anticipate. For example, when you mention to the board that you want to hire a new full-time employee in the spring, the board may advise you to hire the employee only after you purchase a certain piece of equipment, which should be done after the close of your fiscal year.

The members of this board are appointed by you, and you remain the president of the board. The members of the board of directors can consist of yourself, maybe your spouse or a trusted coworker, and one outside person you trust, such as a consultant. Consider having at least one outside person on your board of directors, someone not directly affiliated with your day-to-day operation, but who knows your type of business. For example, if you are in the aircraft job shop business, be sure this person understands the complexity of your operations. This person can help draw your attention to problems, issues, and ideas you may not have thought about.

If you're just starting out in business you won't pay these board members any salary, although you may decide to take them to dinner after each meeting as guests of your company. However, as your company grows, remember that these people helped it grow by offering professional advice. Therefore, you might pay your board members a percentage of your company's annual profit.

The key to keeping a successful board of directors is this: take their advice, and remember that you are one of the voting members on the board! Give your company's board of directors the authority and responsibility to help you direct your company toward future success.

Family-Owned and Operated Businesses

Many small machine shops are owned by a family. A family-owned business can easily and successfully compete with other businesses, yet it presents certain opportunities and problems not found in other businesses.

Management—Don't put family members in charge of others, or in charge of departments, unless they have the right skills. If you do, you lose your experts and cause anger and distrust among those employees who have the potential to move up in the company. Hire family members and make them work their way to the top. Put a family member in charge only when he or she exhibits the knowledge or leadership skills that warrant this responsibility.

Family Members on Teams—If you are working toward a team environment, teams can be an excellent training ground for family members who are new to the business. However, family members on teams present the possible drawback of having others defer to them because of the "inside track" they have to the company's owner. This can inhibit the team from coming up with its own creative ideas. Also, the team may give up if team members feel one person on the team can sabotage their success, so it might be wise to not allow the family member to talk to you about fellow team members. If you do have a family member participating as a team member, be certain to give credence to the team and not the family member on the team.

Decisions are More Critical—It's more difficult to make corporate decisions. Family members frequently raise more objections when the owner attempts to set policy, develop plans, or devise schemes for taking his company into the future. However, having additional family members in the business is an advantage if the family members are united and support each other. The lines of authority and communication must be clear and respected.

(cont.)

■ **Family-Owned and Operated Businesses...**(continued) ■

Difficulty in Dividing Business from Family—One common problem every businessperson faces is how to divide business from family. When you see a family member you work with at a family gathering, it's tempting to discuss business. When you see a family member at work, it's tempting to discuss family matters. You don't want to demonstrate any favoritism to the family member at work, or carry a family argument into the office. As much as possible, keep your family issues at home and your work issues in the shop.

But keep in mind that people tend to work harder—even family members—when the line between business and family is somewhat blurred. For example, when employees are allowed to make some personal telephone calls from work, or bring a project from home to work and work on it after hours, using company equipment, they feel that their work is supporting their home life. They are therefore more apt to bring work home to help meet a deadline, or work overtime to finish a project. This sometimes has to be allowed on a case-by-case basis, but the idea is to be flexible when these requests are made. However, you have to draw the line—especially with family members—if too much advantage is taken of the workplace.

In general, treat family members as you would any employee. Don't expect more or less out of them.

■ Working *On* Your Business

Why is it necessary for you to have vision, mission, strategy, and goals? Because you want to be in control of your business. You want your business to support you. If you want to be the top person who oversees and directs operations, take steps to make your business work for you. Don't work in your business; work *on* your business.

Listen to what Bill Gates, chairman and CEO of Microsoft Corporation, has to say: "Just because someone with a calculator recently deemed me the richest businessman in the world doesn't mean I'm a genius.

"My success in business has largely been the result of my ability to focus on long-term goals and ignore short-term distractions. Taking a long-term view doesn't require brilliance, but it does require dedication.

"As a leader, you must constantly ask yourself: Did I build that technology so it works long-term? Is that customer relationship long-term? Is my distribution strategy long-term? Is the way I set up salaries and incentives inside the company something that will work in the long run?" ("Setting long-term goals key to successful business." The New York Times, 19 July 1995)

You can take control of your business by establishing a long-term view of your shop's future. Your machine shop is your creative enterprise. The future demands your full attention if you are going to make your business work. So, put up your tools, lock up the rollaway, and give all those paper shuffling tasks to those who should be doing them. Once you have your shop working for you, you may even be able to take those extended vacations and extra days off.

CASE STUDY   In 1993 Duane Casa bought a Bridgeport mill and a small lathe, and began machining parts in his garage for a good friend who owned a large job shop. After several months Duane saved enough money to put a down payment on a CNC mill. Within two years Duane had outgrown his garage and moved to a small shop behind a garage on the edge of town. A short time later he moved into a 7000 square foot shop in an industrial area of a nearby city.

Duane now had over 25 employees. He was constantly looking for good, qualified machinists. He was also buried in sales, quotes, and planning. His employees were asking about improved benefits, vacations, sick leave, and overtime pay. Production scheduling was becoming hit and miss, and customers were beginning to respond unfavorably to late deliveries. Quality wasn't as good as Duane had once had it—the type of quality he had built his reputation on. No one who worked for Duane doubted his ability and competence. He really knew the business. But Duane found himself letting important problems slide by in order to solve the more important problems. He just couldn't keep up.

(cont.)

Duane soon realized he would have to turn some of the many functions he was performing over to others. This was hard for him to do. Duane felt that to maintain control he had to stay on top of sales, oversee every quote that went through the shop, and plan each job to run exactly the way he wanted it to run. He found it difficult to let another person step in and "take over" a portion of his business.

Early in 1996 Duane's wife forced him to take a vacation—the first vacation he had had in three years. He hated leaving the shop and did everything he could to avoid going on the vacation. But his wife was insistent, so Duane put one of his most trusted employees in charge of the business and went on vacation.

During this time away from the shop, Duane made some major decisions. He realized that he needed to focus on his business as a whole—where it was going and how it would get there. He saw that there were too many details in business for one person to manage. Duane divided his company into four major parts: sales, planning, office, and production control. He then established specific procedures for each of these four areas, writing out in detail the functions and operations of each.

When Duane returned from vacation, the first thing he did was to hire a salesman. He gave the salesman the mandate he had written and told him to go to work. Next, he placed a long-time assistant in charge of the office and human resources. He hired a planner he knew, and put one of his trusted employees in charge of production control.

Duane quickly found that attitudes seemed to improve. There was a new enthusiasm in the shop. His people knew what he expected, and the heads of his departments had the authority and responsibility to carry out his directives. Quality returned to a high level, and the shop resumed its reputation for excellence.

Duane was more relaxed. His business only needed occasional monitoring. He finally had the time to focus on long-term goals and envision the best ways to make his business successful. He started planning a team environment.

Chapter Summary

- Develop your three key qualities: intelligence, creativity, and follow-through.
- Use these personal qualities to determine your shop's vision, mission, strategy, and goals.
- Select a board of directors to be your advisors.
- Learn to work on your business from your top position, focusing on long-term objectives.

Chapter 3
Managing Change in Your Organization

■ Before You Begin

To move a shop forward toward profit and expansion, a business owner or manager must often make significant changes. That's why you must have a clear picture in your mind of where you want to take your business. In one sense, a business is never finished; it is an ever-changing process. Yet you must know how your business will "feel" when it's become a top shop, what types of processes you'll have in place to effectively handle challenges, and what your customers and others will think when they hear your company name.

Once you embark on making changes in your company, you will start to see a pattern called the Expectation Cycle, or Change Cycle.

■ The Expectation Cycle

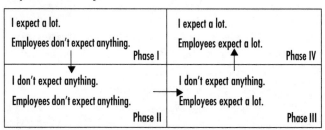

Working through major changes is difficult for any company. But every company that wants to bring about positive and lasting change must begin this journey in much the same way as illustrated in this diagram.

The cycle begins in the upper-left corner. You, the manager, might draw out a plan of what you want your business to look like. You may even list the changes in a step-by-step order that you want to see take place. You may have invested in new equipment, redesigned the offices and shop, and purchased new tools to help convince everyone that a major change—a corporate "paradigm shift"—is on the way.

At this stage, you expect a lot. Your shop personnel and office people, however, don't expect anything. Don't be discouraged by their lack of interest and support. It is difficult for others to immediately share your vision and enthusiasm, even if you've carefully explained it to them.

Part of the problem is that it's all too common for machinists and others to have had bad experiences in the past in which a shop owner or manager had high expectations for success but offered no support to those who actually produced the product. There was a critical imbalance in the workplace. When this occurred, shop workers became dissatisfied and supervisors frustrated. Worker dissatisfaction was expressed by continual employee turnover, poor quality workmanship indicated by a high scrap rate, griping, and anger. Morale was diminished. People became easily irritated by small occurrences and provoked each other. And supervisors probably blamed problems on "incompetent" workers. If your employees have had this type of experience, they will look at your new plans in a negative light.

If you do become discouraged about your plans for the future at this point, what generally occurs next is a loss of your vision. You move to the second part of the Expectation Cycle, the box in the lower-left corner of the illustration. At this stage, you don't expect anything. Neither do the machinists and operators. This is perhaps the lowest, most disappointing level, especially because it follows on the heels of your high expectations.

It's in this second part of the cycle that most managers cease to manage. Hope seems to disappear here. The tendency is that you might give up your plan, abandon your vision, shrug your shoulders, and just let things happen. After all, your expectations were met with everything from ambivalence to fierce resistance. You may begin to allow people to get away with doing little. It can reach a point where making demands has no effect. You may give up and just say, "Well, this is the way people are. I can't change them."

At this low level in the change cycle, workers blame all company problems on the incompetent supervisor or the not-so-smart owner. And the owner wonders how and why so many poor machinists were hired! Unfortunately, it's at this level of the cycle that most shops fail, and most plans to turn the shop around are abandoned.

The key here is to persevere. At this level, *you must put all your attention into supporting your front-line people,* including the machinists, operators, deburrers, and on down the line, encouraging, guiding, and coaching them and paying less attention to the overall plan you hope to initiate.

When the machinists and operators on the front line begin to feel you are behind them, the company begins to push through to the third level (lower-right corner) of the Expectation Cycle. Here you still do not expect anything—you haven't had a chance to concentrate on implementing your vision because there has been too much unrest—but those who work for you have begun to expect a lot.

At this stage, they've come to appreciate the attention they've received. You acknowledged them for decreasing the scrap rate. You started buying high quality cutters to replace the cheap junk they've been using. You praised them on a great tooling design and setup. They are beginning to know you. They're beginning to see their place in your vision.

When this occurs you have turned a major corner. If your support has been consistent, those on the front line will begin to expect a lot of themselves and of you. They will feel closer to management and begin to understand the direction you want them to take. In fact, they often begin going in the right direction before you notice, and in this way, begin to take leadership for the change.

Quite often a manager has been so distressed by his own low expectations and disappointments, he may at first fail to see that he has won over the shop. Suddenly things begin going smoothly.

There's a new friendliness and eagerness in the workplace. When you understand the dynamics that have taken place—that your entire shop has moved into the final part of the Expectation Cycle— change can be effectively implemented. Here you can expect a lot, and the shop expects a lot, too. At long last, your business is moving forward.

The Ideal Balance

When you have reached the fourth level of the Expectation Cycle, your shop will be in balance, operating at its maximum efficiency. You will be the top person in a machine shop that expects top performance from workers, and you will be there to support them. In this situation, a manager gives guidance, makes sure everyone has the tools needed to do his work, and shows interest in daily progress. He talks to his people about the company in general and about job specifics. He's eager to share information about what's going on, and he requests feedback on how *he* is doing.

The result is an immediate increase in productivity. This means greater profit. More importantly, your shop will be ready to make the big changes you have in mind.

CASE STUDY   Jim Brautigan worked as a systems engineer for a large job shop when he was promoted to plant foreman. The plant was under contract to manufacture computer disk drive housings.

The plant Jim took charge of was a disaster. Parts in every possible stage of completion were stacked in every corner of the shop. Many of these parts were not identified as to what stage of production they were in. Weekly production—which should have been 750 housings—was in the range of 350 to 500 housings. The customer was calling daily for parts, angry that everything was so far behind schedule. Quality was at an all-time low.

Jim knew that current management techniques were poor to non-existent. The previous foreman had been brought up through the ranks and had no prior management skills or training. It was common practice in the company to give orders and

(cont.)

then demand results. There was no support or encouragement given to anyone who tried to accomplish something worthwhile. As soon as Jim walked into the plant, the manufacturing manager handed Jim a list of people in the plant that were considered trouble-makers, hoping Jim would fire them.

Jim wanted to turn the operation around and make it a success. He knew he was facing an uphill battle, almost an impossible battle. He was in Phase I of the Expectation Cycle.

The first thing Jim did when he took over the plant was to privately meet with each of the 32 workers in the plant. Employees complained to Jim about low morale. They admitted hiding from supervisors to avoid confrontations. They hid discrepant parts in piles with little or no documentation as to what the discrepancy was. It was safer, they said, to hide a part than to document its flaws.

After he had finished talking to the employees, Jim threw away the to-be-fired list. He knew that firing people was not the solution. Jim was moving into Phase II of the Expectation Cycle.

Jim realized that the only way to turn things around—to successfully meet the weekly production schedule—was to get those in the shop behind him. Those on the front line knew what was wrong. They knew what the problems were, and how they could be solved.

Over the next month Jim solicited the support of the people and attentively listened to their ideas. He let the machinists go ahead with ideas about improving the process. He began to organize and implement some of the broader changes that were suggested to him. He put three full-time machinists to work analyzing the piles of discrepant parts, finding out what stages of development they were in and scheduling them for repairs.

Jim worked hard. The shop worked hard. Production schedules were still not met. The customer kept calling and complaining. The pressure on Jim was great, but he refused to give up and continued the process he had started. The operation was moving into Phase III of the Expectation Cycle.

Suddenly, the changes Jim had worked to implement began to show results. The production schedule was met beyond everyone's expectations—850 quality disk drive housings in one week. Of course, many of these housings were reclaimed parts that had previously been cast aside. The following week the production schedule was met again. Jim overheard employees muttering, "It's about time."

(cont.)

But Jim wasn't quite sure they had turned the corner. The new feeling of cooperation, the excitement, the new sense of purpose, the happy customer, and especially the number of parts produced each week might all be temporary.

Jim continued to work hard. So did the machinists. The plant was entering Phase IV of the Expectation Cycle.

Within two months the plant production had reached an all-time high of over 1500 housings per week. And all without firing anyone. The owner of the company was ecstatic, and gave Jim an unexpected bonus. The manufacturing manager commented to Jim, "I don't know how you did it. You did things I wouldn't have done, and they apparently worked."

Jim wasn't quite sure how he did it either. He persevered. He demonstrated leadership. He knew that he had to gain the trust of the employees because good employees are the key to any successful operation. When the employees in the shop saw what Jim was trying to accomplish—without pointing fingers and giving blame—they got behind him. Before Jim knew it, the employees had turned the shop around.

■ Changing the Company Culture

Changing the shape of your business usually requires more than just making a few changes here and there. Often a company's culture—"the way things are done around here"— must be changed. As an example, when a company decides to form teams to increase performance, it is a major "cultural" change that will take time and patience to bring about.

Your company's culture can be seen in many events and activities. For example, when you come to work in the morning, pour a cup of coffee, visit with coworkers, this is part of your company's culture. Of course, the company culture is much more than socializing. It's the whole company, from sales to production to profit. It's the way coworkers treat each other, how you are treated, and the expectations you have for each other. It includes the attitude workers and the public have toward the company, and the way all things operate within the company.

It takes patience and insight to change a company's culture. For example, you never want to disrupt things that work, so you have to know why certain things work and why other things don't. In order to revise your company's culture, the corporate vision must be freely shared so that each person can understand the reason behind the changes. Each person must visualize his place in the future so that everyone feels secure.

This is one of the major tasks of the top person. You must successfully communicate your vision—the why and wherefore behind the changes. It is vital that everyone knows change is coming, otherwise people will perceive change as chaos. When they see change as chaos they will not recognize each step toward change as a rung on a ladder leading to better management and increased productivity. They may erroneously interpret the change as a frantic effort on the part of the owner or manager to keep the company from sinking.

If you decide to reorganize your machine shop—for example, if you decide to move from a managerial hierarchy to a team environment—consider making layoffs first. This is a painful process for you as well as for supervisors and their subordinates. By making the dramatic changes first, you reassure those remaining that their jobs are secure during the change process. Otherwise they will resist change.

■ The Management of Change

Change is difficult for many people to accept. It takes skill to *prepare* people for change. Usually when people think about change they wonder, "How will the change affect me? Will the change be permanent, or just another flash in the pan?" Each person must be given assurances that he will not lose his job, the company will continue to grow even during the change process, and the final outcome will be an integrated workplace where everyone will be focused toward the same goals. People will work closely in an environment where fresh ideas and insights can be put to use.

People look forward to change when they have input regarding how the change is to take place and an investment in the final outcome. This doesn't mean that the details of all your plans must be discussed with everyone and put to a popular vote. It means that everyone should know major changes are going to occur and should be assured of their continued value to the company.

In general, people go through a process of accepting change similar to the steps listed below. You can take action each step of the way through the change process, thereby effectively preparing your employees for change. Managing change means removing your employee's fears and helping them focus on how beneficial the change will be.

Reactions to Change	What the Manager Can Do
The first reaction to change is generally positive. A person usually says, "I'm confident and look forward to change. I'm excited. It's about time things changed around here."	As manager, your response to this first reaction is to help the employee look down the road. First, you should show your appreciation for his enthusiasm. But then, gently direct his focus away from the immediate change and help him see the big picture. Prepare him for the long-term process of change.
After the initial enthusiasm wears off, the second reaction to change is often pessimistic. Afterthoughts set in. People begin to wonder if the old ways weren't better. They begin to have misgivings, such as, "I wonder if I'm going to be expected to produce the same number of parts and record all this SPC data at the same time. Maybe I can't cope with the changes. Maybe it will embarrass me in front of others."	These are realistic fears. Be sure to sit with each individual and discuss his apprehension with him. As manager, address these misgivings by asking the individual what he can do about his thoughts and feelings. Maybe he has some ideas so ask for them. Let him talk. Talking eases fears. We all realize that nothing is as bad as we thought after we have a chance to talk about it. After the person has talked openly to you, explain that apprehension is part of the change process and that you are there to help him through the changes. That's part of your job.

(cont.)

Reactions to Change	What the Manager Can Do
The third reaction to change is usually realistic. A person says to himself, "I'm beginning to see that the changes taking place might work after all. I'm settling in. Things might not be so bad."	When this occurs, talk to the individual about what he has accomplished thus far. Be very clear in your praise for what he has done to help changes take place. Let him see how important his accomplishments are and how they're a vital part of the overall growth process. When a person sees that his work has been part of the change process all along, he will be much more relaxed and confident about events.
The fourth reaction to change is growing confidence. The person might say, "The fruits of my labor are beginning to show."	Talk to the individual and offer encouragement. But remind him that he's not home free. There's more to come. Change takes time, and change has now become part of the company's big game plan. There's no going back. There's only the future and it takes perseverance to get there.
Finally, there is general acceptance to change.	Deal with this by asking your employee, "What did you do to achieve this?" Let him explain his thoughts and feelings about the entire process. Help him see that he played an important part in the new developments. By giving him a chance to articulate the effect the entire change process had on him, he begins to openly support the new way of doing things, and he will help in the "fine-tuning" that may yet be required.

Responding to Negative Reactions to Change

Change always produces some negative reactions that won't go away. A few people will be critical of the process, regardless if the change is a minor adjustment, such as purchasing a new CNC machine or repainting the office, or a major shift in company policy.

Few people have the vision necessary to see the big picture, to see themselves in the big picture. Their frequent comments can cause general hard feelings among coworkers. Besides, many people see change as interfering with their daily work. After all, they want to get things done, and when changes take place, their work can be interrupted.

As a manager who is about to initiate a change in organization that will increase productivity, and therefore profit, you must decide how important it is for you to respond to workers who don't want change to occur. If you want to head off as much resistance as possible, consider this: In the long run it's better to take steps to get everyone on the side of change, rather than ignore the negative comments and let resistance to change eat away at all you are trying to achieve.

Of course you can always fire those who don't want to go with the program. But it's more expensive to fire and hire someone new than it is to train the people you have. From a purely economic viewpoint, firing a person should always be the very, very last option. More importantly, if you can turn around opposition so that the opposition now supports you, you have the strongest ally possible. You can enlist this ally in the onward development of your organization.

A negative reaction means firm resistance. Don't take negative reactions lightly! How should you respond? When one of your people resists change and makes negative comments about it, the first thing to do is to listen to him. Then find a way to talk him through his reservations.

| **CASE STUDY** | Jana Bergman operated a CNC machining center that was producing bow risers for an archery company. Besides receiving an hourly wage, she was paid an incentive on quotas. At the end of |

each shift, the risers were counted and she was paid an addi-

(cont.)

tional dollar amount for everything she produced above a certain quantity.

Her foreman announced one day that the company was going to install a pallet changer on her machine, which would result in speeding up the machining process. This was good news, the foreman insisted, because more risers would be produced and the quota would remain the same.

Jana disliked the idea. She complained and sought to get others on her side. She wanted to fight the idea.

Her foreman approached her one day and asked her to join him in the lunchroom. Jana thought for sure she was going to be fired. She was surprised when her foreman bought her a soft drink, sat with her at one of the tables, and asked, "Jana, what can I do to get you behind the new pallet changer idea? You're a valuable person to the company and everyone looks up to you. I'd really like your support."

Jana was stunned. She didn't think her boss cared for her views. She was almost embarrassed when she said, "Well, I thought it was going to force us to work harder."

Her boss laughed. "You work hard enough already! The purpose of installing the pallet changer is so you can load the next set of parts while the machine is running. You won't have to stop the machine to do that. You have plenty of time between cycles. Believe me, you'll make more money with this new innovation. I know you will, because you're already one of my star producers."

Here's a list of the most common reasons why a person fears or dislikes change. Your employees may make comments such as:

- I am afraid of losing power.
- I know what should be done, but no one listens to me.
- I have seniority, but now I'll lose it.
- The changes will make me look foolish.
- I'm old-fashioned. I won't be able to adapt to these new-fangled ways.
- I'll lose my new desk or workstation.
- The goals are unclear. I'm confused.
- Communication will be poor. I won't know what's going on.
- Everyone won't be involved. I'll look silly making the changes by myself.

- I don't trust the people making this change. They don't know what they're doing.
- I'm satisfied with the way things are. Why do they have to change anything?
- What do I get after the changes are made? More problems and more work?
- I'll just have to work harder. There will be more pressure.
- I might fail.
- I've seen changes before. They don't work.
- The change will be too rapid. They're expecting too much too soon.
- No one really supports this change.
- Change will create conflicting priorities. No one will know what we're supposed to do.
- We'll be driven by a schedule, goals, and efficiency experts. It won't be a nice place to work anymore.
- I don't think the boss is really committed.

These are very real fears or concerns people have when faced with changes.

Here's the best way to remove a person's fear. First, talk to him about his opposition to change. Let him express frustration. In most instances that will solve the problem because he will be satisfied with the chance to state his opinion. If the person still continues voicing negative comments about the changes taking place, you must determine the source of his resistance or you won't have peace in your company.

Try to get the person to talk with you about the change process again. If he doesn't offer a reason for his resistance, is reluctant about discussing it with you, or is vague and inconsistent, select any of the fears from the list and ask if this is the thinking behind his opposition. For example, you can ask, "Do you think the change will diminish your position in the company?"

Whether he responds "yes" or "no," offer a solution to the fear you expressed on his behalf. For instance, respond by saying, "You're valuable to the company. That won't change."

If he insists that you're on the wrong track, that what you're saying has nothing to do with his resistance to change, select another fear from the list of common fears, express it, and offer your solution. Remember, you want him to confess to the real reason behind his negative comments. Therefore, continue by saying, "If this problem were solved, how would you respond?" If he insists you're on the wrong track he may tell you why he opposes the change. If you're on the right track, he'll answer your question.

Continue to probe until you uncover the real source of resistance! Even try inventing an outlandish reason for his negative response to change. As an example, you might ask, "Are you afraid you'll lose your vacation pay?" What this does is lighten the pressure. Hopefully he will tell you what his real fears are.

If you have tried everything and you still cannot help him dissolve his fears, consider whether his negative reactions are tearing down the change process and inciting fears in others. If they are not, just let things go for awhile. You can tackle the problem again later. He may change his attitude as things progress, and he will always appreciate that you made the effort to talk with him.

However, if his negative reaction is causing disruption, and you've probed and cannot get to the bottom of his bitterness, you must take him aside and be very frank. Tell him what his actions are doing. Explain how he is disrupting things and how his attitude and behavior make the changes more difficult for everyone. Insist that he bring all negative comments to you and no one else.

Tell him you want to hear all his complaints. Explain that maybe both of you together can do something about the difficulties he perceives. Get down to basics with him. Otherwise, persistent negative comments will result in a no-growth situation.

Chapter Summary

- Before you start making changes, prepare yourself by understanding the Expectation Cycle.
- Change the company culture by sharing your vision of the company's future.
- Manage change and fight resistance to change by being open to your employees' concerns and frankly addressing them.

Chapter 4
Supporting
Your Employees

■ Unleashing the Potential

It's an odd thing about competition. If you don't have a competitor, you soon will have. If you offer a low price, someone will offer a lower price. If you offer quick service, someone will offer quicker service. If you offer a solution to every problem, someone will claim to have a better solution for every problem.

What moves any organization past its competitors is the creative dynamics of its people. If you unleash the potential of your employees—that is, if you allow them to become experts, attentive to quality, efficiency, and on-time deliveries, and professional in every way—your organization will immediately begin to blaze new trails right past your competitors.

Perhaps the first change you need to work on is in how you relate to your employees. Managers must work with people, not products or services. Once a manager has established the company's vision and mission, and broken them down into strategies and goals, he must go about implementing his plans. But he must rely on his people to do it. No matter how excellent a technician a manager is, or once was, if he cannot work well with people, he cannot get results from them and his company will not remain competitive.

Results are the "bottom line" of being in business. If the manager doesn't get the expected results, he has failed. No amount of cajoling, threats, or displays of anger and frustration on the part of the manager will make a worker produce the required results. In fact, it will have the opposite effect. When a manager flails his arms about, yelling and screaming, and belittles those he hired to do the job, he loses their respect. When a manager resorts to bribery to get results ("Finish this by noon today, Ed, then take the rest of the day off with pay"), people will begin working for bribes. When a manager resorts to placing responsibility for some problem on a third party ("Production control screwed up again!"), this only serves to alienate people from each other, when they should be working together.

To unleash potential and get the right results, a manager must support his people by being aware of what they need to do their jobs, helping them stay focused on their task, and removing obstacles that keep them from excelling.

■ Performance Needs

A person is hired to perform specific services for the company. His success, therefore, depends on how well that service is performed. For example, machinists are hired to machine parts, to carry out and fulfill tasks in a certain way. The role of management is to support the machinist so he can accomplish his tasks. A business makes money when front-line workers produce at peak levels, when they perform their services well.

To produce at peak levels, a front-line worker needs three things:

1. Training
2. Tools
3. Information about how he is doing, or feedback

Everyone requires training so he knows how to do his job. He needs the right tools, and he must be told the good news and the bad news about how he is doing.

The Danger of Overhead

When a machine shop begins to succeed the manager some-times hires too many people in an effort to meet peak demand. When demand levels out, the company is stuck with "fat" it has built during a time of high growth. It is not uncommon for a machine shop owner to land a big contract, buy some addi-tional equipment, hire more help, then have to lay people off when the contract runs out.

Everyone above the machinists, machine operators, and shop personnel are considered "overhead." Overhead can be dan-gerous because it's expensive. An employee must either make the company money by earning his own salary, or save the company more money than he is being paid.

Even worse than having overhead is the barrier excessive overhead creates between front-line workers and the owner. When you have too much overhead, supervisors sometimes sim-ply watch workers work. They might watch over the shoulders of lower level workers. Sometimes they hold "meetings," which are nothing but another way to watch others work. To pay people to watch people is costly and produces nothing of value.

A good manager, although he constitutes overhead, can save a company money. He can be a valuable asset to a company if he knows his job and is successful at keeping those he man-ages productive.

Here's the key: pare the company down, keeping the best people you have. If you must lay people off because too much fat has been accumulated during times of growth, you must evaluate your employees and make fair decisions about who to let go. Following is a good rule-of-thumb evaluation:

- Aptitude. Does the employee have the aptitude or talent required by his position? Can he "grow" into his job, and grow with the company? Does he demonstrate intelligence, creativity, and follow-through?
- Attitude. Does the employee demonstrate a positive atti-tude toward the company? Does he get along with co-workers? Does he enjoy working with others?
- Attentiveness. Is the employee attentive to what he is do-ing? Does he make lots of mistakes? Is he careless with his work?
- Attendance. Is the employee at work every day? Does he show up on time?

(cont.)

The Danger of Overhead...(continued)

These four A's—aptitude, attitude, attentiveness, and atten-dance—are often the key qualities to consider. Decide which of these are most valuable to you, and then try to be as objective as possible.

Once you've trimmed down your shop to a reasonable size, formulate a plan to meet a steep incline in business should one arise. With your support, your employees will be able to meet this demand.

▪ Basic Needs Everyone Has

In addition to the need for training, tools, and feedback, every person has a basic need to be treated with respect and to have his ideas listened to. When a person's idea is heard, it's a confirmation that he is a valued employee. It means he is a vital part of the group. Even if the individual is not given direct credit for the idea, to see his idea take shape gives value to his life. He has contributed a part of himself. Optimism and enthusiasm increase proportionally when a person sees his ideas have taken root in others' actions.

Work is not just earning a paycheck. In many ways it's part of a person's self-worth—how he sees himself. A sharp boss who understands this helps employees develop toward their maximum potential. He listens attentively, then makes decisions that help the employees on their journey toward success. This isn't done out of pure altruism; it's good for business. When a person grows in his job, he either makes the company money or saves the company money.

Even if your company has hired an employee for a menial task—such as cleaning the shop floor—and all this employee looks forward to is clocking in his eight hours and then getting out of there, you can sit with him a moment, find out his interests, and offer some form of encouragement that may ultimately change his attitude. You never know what may result. Many times leaders of great companies have started out on the very bottom rung of the ladder.

Of course not all ideas are good. Not all good ideas are timely, and not all timely ideas are smart. You working alone, or the teams you create, must decide which ideas are worth implementing or exploring. Few people are irrational enough to demand that their ideas, or their way of doing things, must take precedence over the good of the shop. So, it never hurts to listen carefully to someone before making a decision.

When a person's ideas are *not* listened to, or given any consideration, quite often the person will begin looking for another job in a shop where people will listen. It's that important.

CASE STUDY   The case of Derek Hightower is not unusual. Derek had jumped from shop to shop for many years, sometimes working only a few months at a shop, then moving on. He liked being a machinist, but never seemed to "fit in." He enjoyed being creative in his approach to machining parts, but his ideas were seldom accepted. A foreman usually has his mind set on how he wants the job run.

When Derek came to work for Nordic Sheet Metal, he stayed there over four years. When asked what was different about Nordic compared to some of the other shops he'd worked in, he answered, "The boss listens. He's not hard to talk with. If you have an idea, you can bring it to him and he shows his appreciation. At Nordic I'm included in the planning process. I'm part of the team, and my ideas are valued. They don't always use my ideas, but they listen, and sometimes they do use my ideas.

"Here's an example. Soon after I started at Nordic I was operating a large press and was having difficulty maintaining a given dimension from the end of the part to the formed angle. Other features of the part prohibited using the end of the part for a reference. I suggested building a special stop to locate the part using holes that had been previously machined, using the end for a reference. My supervisor liked the idea and had the special stop made. It worked great!"

▪ The Organization as a Pyramid

You can gain a better understanding of how to support your employees by comparing several visual models for organizations, and seeing where you fit into them.

The traditional model for an organization is based on a pyramid, as shown in the accompanying diagram. A management pyramid begins to develop the moment the top person hires the first employee. When others are hired the management pyramid quickly grows. Each person hired brings many talents into the company, as well as many problems.

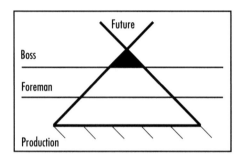

In the pyramid, the shop owner or manager who receives information and issues commands is at the pyramid's apex. His next in command, whether a vice-president or supervisor, ranks just below the top level, occupying an upper portion of the pyramid, and so forth on down the pyramid. Those who perform the actual work—the planners, programmers, machinists, deburr people and so on—are frequently depicted along the pyramid's base. They are the ones who make money for the company, and in the pyramid illustration, support everyone above them.

What's good about viewing your top position using the pyramid analogy is that it gives a clear picture of who is in charge of whom, and where the division of labor begins and ends. Besides, the pyramid is an ancient symbol and has successfully been used to illustrate corporate structure for centuries. However, it can negatively reflect your attitude to your employees—that is, it can imply that you look down on them.

Consider these other negative connotations associated with a pyramid:

1. A pyramid is inflexible.
2. A pyramid is a construct, not an organic process, so it cannot grow.
3. Once built, a pyramid cannot be easily moved or changed.
4. Whatever does not fit into the pyramid structure is often discarded.

5. The base of the pyramid is excessively large in order to support the apex.
6. It is difficult to climb the pyramid.

▪ The Organization as a Tree

Considering the pyramid's characteristics, perhaps it is not the best model for your company. Is it possible to find a different model that will correctly convey your supportive nature and the qualities you want your shop to possess? Keeping in mind the same business functions illustrated in the pyramid, apply these functions to a tree.

Consider these tree characteristics:

1. A tree is flexible. It's built to bend, not break.
2. A tree is organic; it grows and develops.
3. Once planted, a tree can easily be pruned and shaped.
4. A tree is able to respond to external forces.
5. A tree frequently allows for sudden and unexpected growth.
6. The roots of the tree supply nourishment to the fruit—the final result.
7. There's no reason to climb a tree; its purpose is to produce fruit.

Using the tree model, the planners, programmers, machinists, deburr people and so on—those who produce the "fruit," or parts your customers order—reside at the top. The smaller branches and the trunk represent various departments or personnel that offer additional support to those who produce the fruit. The roots represent the owner, the main support of this living organization, well planted in the world of business for a strong foundation. It is from the roots that the tree derives nourishment. It is your job to make certain everyone involved in producing fruit receives the proper nurturing and nourishment necessary to excel. When everyone receives what they need to do their jobs, then you can begin to concentrate on the future by exploring new ways to make your machine shop grow naturally.

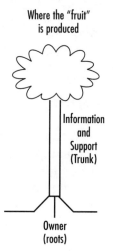

Where the "fruit" is produced

Information and Support (Trunk)

Owner (roots)

In this age of exploding technology, narrow profit margin, and higher customer demands, the pyramid model does not fit the adaptability requirements needed today. It is not flexible enough to meet new challenges. It is too structured, too slow to adjust to new technology and trends. Although the tree model may seem somewhat cliche, it is actually a more accurate picture of how you should view your organization and your place in it. When viewed as a tree, your business is able to bend, to take advantage of economic winds, put out new branches, explore new avenues, develop or adapt to new technology, and quickly and comfortably establish new relationships with clients. And you become the supportive base for all of this healthy activity.

■ The Organization as a Brain

Another model you can use to visualize your company is a brain. As a brain, your machine shop is able to obtain all the knowledge it can about the marketplace and technology, and can use that knowledge to make new products, enter new niches, and direct your output toward customer needs. To work smart, you must go beyond technology. Your machine shop, and all those in it, must be attuned to the times, to economic trends, to customer needs, and to each other.

Knowledge flow never stops. It doesn't matter where the knowledge comes from—an employee, a trade publication, a casual comment dropped by a customer—if it is right, if it is smart, if your company is a brain, it can use that knowledge for profitability.

Knowledge also brings an end to the command-and-control environment. You are still in charge, but you are working *with* the employees, not against them. It is not a large jump to see the value in sharing insights and information with everyone. This is because individuals at every level in a shop environment are skilled people with insights. Technological skills at all levels are more refined than they ever were in the past. When you turn your shop into a brain, it assimilates new skills as it needs them. A successful manager builds on the differing skills and potential of his employees, using knowledge to advance his business.

Sharing knowledge and concerns with employees and encouraging them to share knowledge with you builds confidence. Confidence increases speed of service and focuses attention on results. Confidence is an invisible superstructure in your shop that a customer wants to see.

When the company is perceived as a brain, intelligence becomes the basic building block. When organizations depend on brains to get things done, they can cut labor costs, quickly adapt to new technology—the software and hardware needed to serve their customers best—assimilate new ideas, define goals, and build relationships that are vital to increased performance and profit.

■ Keeping Employees Focused

Every job at every level consists of important and unimportant activities. In other words, regardless of what we do, we cannot be "on task" 100% of the time. Everyone has to take time out to think things through, maybe chart a new course, or rearrange a workstation. Yet it should be everyone's job—including your job as manager—to know which tasks are important and which aren't, and to *whom* they're important.

When a worker is focused on a task, he immediately begins to master it. Once he gains mastery, he can begin to experiment. To work with concentration and enthusiasm opens the door to creativity: innovation, simplification, discovery of unforeseen relationships between tasks, and generation of new ideas, shortcuts, and unexpected results.

Think of a child at play. He doesn't play long at one task before he begins to innovate. He begins to make new rules for the "game." He begins to test ideas against results. But a child doesn't do this before he has mastered a basic task.

For example, a child plays in the sandbox. His first task is to fill his pail with sand. He might fill it several times, dig it out again, and fill it again. He might pack it tightly, then try to pry it loose with a stick or shovel. He does this until he has convinced himself he has mastered the art of pail packing.

When he's mastered packing the pail with sand, what does he usually do next? He begins to experiment. He might turn the pail upside-down and carefully lift the pail in an attempt to remove the sand to form a perfect cone shape. This new task may occupy him for some time.

The lesson is this: there is a three-step process of focusing, mastering, then developing. This is the key to becoming a creative master of any skill, whether painting a picture, playing the piano, or becoming a basketball star:

1. *Focus* on the task as much as possible, to the exclusion of all else.
2. *Master* the task, becoming more than proficient. Become an expert.
3. *Develop* the task. Move beyond mastery to innovation.

Remember, however, that focus and mastery of tasks must be the first priority. As the owner or manager of a business, it is your responsibility to see that everyone sticks with these first two steps most of the time. You have specific tasks you must perform. Likewise, you hire machinists to perform specific tasks, such as machining parts as planned and programmed. You must convince the employees that performing a task well and making or saving the company money is far more important than being creative and ingenious just for the sake of being creative and ingenious. Your company's overriding goal is to financially succeed, to make a profit. Few companies have the financial leeway that allows machinists, for example, to experiment and be innovative in the middle of a production run.

▪ The Danger of Taking Over Tasks

Occasionally, employees will fail to do their tasks properly or efficiently. Your first inclination may be to jump in and take over. But you will soon discover that taking on tasks when systems fail is not the solution. You will only confuse the issues, and you'll be headed for overload. Doing others' jobs will get you embroiled deeper in the problems and will never allow you time to work *on* the business. Plus, you are not really supporting your employees this way, because you're not allowing them to learn from their mistakes and solve their own problems.

CASE STUDY   Matt Rains is president of All-Max, Inc., a prime aircraft job shop. Recently, a series of quotes by the estimator went through the system. The quotes were submitted to the customer and the contracts were awarded to the company based on those quotes. Upon careful review by various department heads, the jobs were found to be seriously underbid, causing the company to lose money on the jobs. In order to avoid such mistakes in the future, Matt asked for all quotes to come to him for approval before submitting them to the customer.

Review the problems Matt created for himself:

1. What's Matt going to do when the programming department starts making mistakes? Is Matt going to have all CNC programs come to him for approval?
2. Is Matt going to do production control when delivery deadlines are missed?

Matt could be a very busy guy. By trying to solve problems himself rather than developing long-range solutions, he won't have time to plan for his business to grow.

What Matt should have done when the estimator missed the quote by such a large margin is to review estimating procedures. Matt could have asked himself questions such as, "Is the right person doing the estimating? Does he possess the necessary skills to perform the tasks? Can I offer some training? Does any other person review these quotes for accuracy?"

When dealing with problems such as these, remember that a good manager doesn't point fingers and look for blame. It doesn't matter too much who created the problem. What must be of greatest concern is how to solve the problem so it won't happen again. Evaluate the situation, and provide the training, tools, and feedback the employee needs so he can solve his problems himself. If you simply take over, you can only become frustrated, frustrate those around you, and ultimately contribute to a sense of failure and lack of confidence.

■ The Support Technique

It's not easy to offer the support people need so they can become top performers. Good support consists of emotional feedback as well as technical guidance. Too often a manager sacrifices one in favor of the other. A manager must carefully strike the balance between coaxing those under his supervision toward improving their technical ability and at the same time helping them develop those "inner" qualities that lead to star performance for all involved.

The more those under a manager's guidance feel the support of upper-level management—when they know the company's behind them—the more they produce. When a machinist does not feel supported by his supervisor, his production immediately decreases. A machine shop cannot survive in days of marginal profits when production or service drops.

Thus, a manager supports his subordinates in order to help them become experts. Experts produce results that lead to profit. (Improving job performance and creating experts will be covered in greater detail in Chapter Nine: Improving Performance.)

Chapter Summary

- ■ Unleash your employees' potential by providing the training, tools, and feedback they must have in order to get results.
- ■ Show your employees how valuable they are by listening to their ideas and concerns.
- ■ See yourself as the supportive "roots" of your organization.

Chapter 5
Critical Relationships

■ Your Critical Relationships

Whether you are the owner of a machine shop, or one of many machinists, there are people who expect you to be a star performer. Everyone who is on top of his profession, and remains there, either intuitively or thoughtfully knows who these individuals in his workplace are, and seeks to improve his relationship with them by meeting their expectations. These relationships are essential to success, which is why they are "critical."

Understanding your critical relationships changes your view of yourself and how you do things. The first step toward success is to *define your success from the viewpoints of these people*. From there, you must assist your employees in determining their critical relationships and defining the expectations those relationships bring. This is one of the most important ways you can actively support your employees.

Not only do these key individuals inside and outside your shop expect things from you, but you will also expect certain things from them. Problems in the infrastructure of a shop usually begin when you don't deliver what is expected of you to one or more of these key individuals, or when you don't receive from them what they should be giving to you.

■ How Critical Relationships Affect Performance

To understand the value of critical relationships in a work environment, think of a person who is a poor performer. We all know such people. Who does the poor performer spend his time with? What relationships does he nurture?

A poor performer usually spends time with those who support and reinforce his poor performance. He attracts people who have time to listen to reasons why he does not do well and who sympathize with him. He frequently blames others—usually those individuals with whom he should be nurturing healthy relationships—for his poor workmanship.

By contrast, think of a successful person, a top performer. Who does he spend his time with? What relationships does he nurture? Who reinforces him?

The star performer spends his time with mentors, seasoned professionals, and others with creative ideas—in other words, with successful people. He exchanges ideas with them and seriously considers what he hears. He stays focused on success by perfecting his own skills. He strives to produce quality results. He measures his success by the achievements and opinions of other star performers.

A star performer knows where he gets his work and where it goes. He is keenly aware of his relationship to each of the persons or companies involved, and knows whether that relationship is improving or deteriorating. His goal is to become an expert at what he does from the viewpoints of his critical relationships.

■ Four Examples of Critical Relationships in Business

The following are the individuals behind the four categories of critical relationships found in every business:

1. Employer
2. Supervisor
3. Customer
4. Supplier

All of the people involved in these four types of critical relationships expect something of each other. As a manager, you must know how to respond to those with whom you have critical relationships. Without giving them what they need, or getting from them what you need, there is no way you can succeed, regardless of how good you are at your job. The same holds true for every person in your shop.

Critical Relationship #1: The Employer

The employer is the one who owns the business. The name of the company is usually closely associated with the employer. As an example, a shop's owner is Jane Allison, and her company's name is All Manufacturing. Those who work for Jane regard All Manufacturing as their employer. If you are the owner of a shop, you are the employer.

In a large corporation, the employer is the person who owns the majority of stock, or perhaps is the chairman of the board of directors. The employer is the one who authorizes someone to pay employees for what they do, signs the checks, and decides how much each employee is worth in terms of wages.

Take a moment to think about an employer's concerns and needs. If you want to help your employees succeed, you have to help them look at their job and the work they do through the employer's eyes, whether or not that person is you. Regardless of his position, the more an individual in a job shop knows what his employer expects, the wider the door is open to individual success for that person.

The employer's main interest is *profit*. That's why he's in business. Profit is money left over after all debts, including salaries, bonuses, etc. have been paid. Since the employer is in business to make a profit, he expects all employees to immediately or eventually help his company bring in a profit. Thus, if someone receives a salary of $50,000 a year, the employer wants to know if that employee is either saving the shop $50,000 a year, or bringing into the company more than $50,000 a year.

Everyone who works at a company must have a job that is vital to the company's present stability and future growth. Therefore, it is essential for each person in the shop to nurture his relationship with his employer. A person doesn't have to personally meet or even get to know his employer. In fact, this may not be possible. But everyone can nurture a relationship with the employer by keeping in mind that he must earn his salary or hourly wage.

Another of the employer's expectations is for everyone to take outspoken pride in the company's achievements. The employer expects workers to give enthusiastic support for the company.

In turn, each employee expects certain things from the employer. An employee expects a certain amount of job security, a nice place to work, and a standard of excellence.

What the employer expects from each employee	What employees expect from the employer
Profit	Job security
Pride in the company	Good working environment
Cost cutting	A standard of excellence

Critical Relationship #2: The Supervisor

Everyone has a supervisor, even the shop's owner! When the owner is his own supervisor, he must hold himself closely to those expectations he has for others. In some cases an owner might regard the board of directors as the supervisor, but that's not quite the same. A board doesn't have the power to fire an owner.

If you are the owner of a shop and also the one to whom everyone reports, you are both *employer* and *supervisor*. This means, of course, that not only are you interested in each person's speed, efficiency, and quality of work, but you're also interested in profit and company pride.

Unlike an employer, everyone in the shop personally knows his immediate supervisor. A supervisor is the person who can hire or fire. He is the one who oversees and reviews other people's work. Because a supervisor can make the life of any employee miserable or happy, it is vitally important for each employee to nurture his relationship with the supervisor! A successful employee does what the supervisor expects, and does it quickly, so the supervisor remains happy and satisfied. If the machinist goes home in the evening and complains to his spouse about how hard he worked, chances are he's made the supervisor happy.

Every supervisor in every type of business has three major concerns. First, the supervisor wants an employee to complete more work so he can take on another assignment. The supervisor also wants the work done quickly, and he wants it done right. Every supervisor is concerned with efficiency, speed, and quality of workmanship.

On the other hand, employees expect certain things from the supervisor. They expect fair treatment, the right tools and equipment so they can do the work, and feedback so they know how they're doing.

Fair treatment means that the supervisor won't give a machinist an impossible or unrealistic task, or have expectations that are beyond his capacity to produce. The proper tools must be the latest and best tools available, or at least the latest technological equipment your shop can afford. Feedback is information about how a person is doing. Without this useful direction, no one can possibly know how or where to make improvements in his work.

Of the four examples of critical relationships in business, the relationship between machinist and supervisor is often the most stressful, challenging, and difficult to nourish. Yet it is the most critical. Unless the supervisor and employee both foster this relationship, the shop as a whole—and the individuals within it—cannot succeed.

If your shop is growing successfully, you will eventually reach a point when you can no longer be both employer and supervisor. You will have to hire someone, or move a technical person up from the ranks, to be the supervisor. In this case, you must train him carefully so he can use those communication skills necessary for getting the most in terms of speed, efficiency, and quality of work out of those he supervises. You, in turn, become his supervisor, and it's up to you to get the same results out of him that he is charged with getting out of others.

What the supervisor expects from his employees	What the employee expects from his supervisor
More work done	Fair treatment
Quality work	Right tools and equipment
Work done faster	Feedback, a good flow of information

Critical Relationship #3: The Customer

For the machine shop as a whole, the customer is the person or organization who receives the product your company makes. Within a machine shop, the customer is the next person down the line, the one who directly receives the product or part an employee makes or service he provides.

Let's first think about the customers who hire your company. These customers are critical to the success of your business because they are the people who pay for the work you do. Without the customer, your company wouldn't exist.

All customers want to know when they can receive the product, how good it is, and how much it costs. These three expectations—schedule, quality, price—are true in every business/customer relationship, including those in the machine shop industry.

Whenever there is competition between shops, the shop that is "customer-driven" is the one that wins out. When a shop commits itself to understanding what the customer needs and giving the greatest service by exceeding expectations in the three major areas, it can quickly outdistance other shops vying for the same customer base.

Your machine shop must strive to excel in all three of these key areas: schedule, price, and quality. Of course, some customers may have higher expectations in one or two of these areas, and lower expectations in the rest. For example, a customer may be willing to pay more and give you more time in order to ensure extremely tight tolerances. However, in order to remain competitive, you must be ready to meet realistically high expectations in all three areas. You cannot place greater priority on one over the others.

Occasionally, you may have to work with a customer on determining realistic, practical expectations. For example, a customer may require dimensional tolerances that seem a bit tight. Their shipping requirements frequently change or may be impossible to implement. Traceability requirements may be too time-consuming or difficult to maintain. If the customer's expectations are truly unrealistic, a good shop will help the customer understand these difficulties and offer solutions.

In addition to expecting the customers to have realistic demands, a shop expects its customers to have confidence in its ability to handle the order, plus an understanding of what the shop is set up to do. The shop expects to be rewarded with repeat business based on good work, and hopes its customers will spread the word about the shop's outstanding service. The best way to get new customers is to take good care of the long-time customers.

What the shop's customer expects	What the shop expects from its customer
Accurate delivery schedule	Confidence in the shop's ability
Appropriate level of quality	Knowledge of the company's mission
Agreed-upon price	Repeat business

Within the shop, however, many individuals have very little or no *direct* relationship with the machine shop's customer. For example, the machinist's customer is the next person down the line from him, the person who receives his output. This is what is known as an "internal" customer.

Nevertheless, some of the same rules hold true for the machinist's customers as they do for the machine shop's customer. The person who receives the machinist's output expects two things from the machinist: quality and prompt delivery.

Just as you must think about your shop's customers' needs, the machinist must think about the needs of the person who receives his output. His success as a machinist, in part, depends upon the professional relationship he develops with that person. For example, the machinist who designs and builds tooling to be used on CNC or other production machines has a critical relationship with his customer—the person who sets up and operates those machines. A poor relationship between these two machinists prevents both of them from becoming successful.

Critical Relationship #4: The Supplier

The same internal and external aspects of customer relationships apply to supplier relationships as well. But, by definition, the supplier is the person or organization that provides the goods and services your company needs to manufacture parts.

Your shop's supplier is a critical relation because without him, your shop won't get what it needs to do the job. When supplies are not delivered on time, or the wrong material is delivered, it puts the shop behind schedule.

The supplier needs three things in order to do his job. He needs enough time to supply the orders, so be sure to place orders in advance. He also needs accurate information on what you want. For example, if your shop's purchasing clerk calls a supplier and says, "Send me some 1/2" 2-flute high-speed end mills," but does not specify single- or double-end, the supplier may not be able to deliver the correct supplies. Therefore, be specific in orders and requests. The supplier also needs occasional feedback. Your supplier doesn't want to lose your shop's business, so be clear on what's expected.

The supplier is often the most misunderstood of all critical relationships. When a supplier doesn't deliver material or parts on time, it's fairly common for many job shop managers to switch to another supplier, even if they made the error of not giving the supplier enough lead time. After all, you may conclude, there are many suppliers out there. I'll find one who is hungry enough to bring me what I need on time! Although it's fair to expect a timely delivery and the right parts from the supplier, it's far wiser to nurture a good relationship with that supplier than to discard the supplier due to an occasional foul-up in an order.

Of course you have to decide if your current suppliers consistently give you the service you require so your shop runs smoothly. Consider keeping your supplier because:

- When your supplier knows your business, because he has done business with you, he knows your requirements from previous orders. This means fewer inventory and shipping errors.
- An established supplier will often give you partial shipments, try to keep your regular order on-hand, and be able to quickly process recurring orders.
- A good supplier is usually more eager to service his established customers because they have demonstrated their reliability.
- He may be willing to extend credit when you have a cash-flow problem.

- An established supplier who knows you will often work harder to shop for the lowest price for you.

As much as possible, keep working with your shop's established suppliers. It takes a lot of energy—often wasted energy—to shop for a new supplier. Besides, there is a learning curve in every business/supplier relationship. Think about how long it will take a new supplier to catch on to how you do business.

Try to avoid an "adversarial" relationship with your supplier. For example, don't offer a very low price on a job and then expect your supplier to lower his prices to help you. If you have unrealistic expectations of your supplier, you will become angry and frustrated and he will resent doing business with you.

What the supplier expects from the shop	What you expect from the supplier
Delivery lead-time	The materials or service ordered
Accurate order description	On-time delivery
Feedback on how he is doing	Agreed-upon price

Once again, a machinist may not have any *direct* relationship with the machine shop's suppliers. He may have nothing to do with ordering parts or raw materials. His supplier is the previous person up the line from him, the person who gives him the part he needs so he can do his job.

In this relationship, the same expectations exist. The machinist expects to receive *on time* what he needs so he can do his job. He also expects to receive the specific material he's supposed to have. And the person up the line, perhaps another machinist, expects to receive enough time to produce the part he passes on to the machinist and feedback on how he is doing.

Therefore, it's vital for the machinist to foster a relationship with his internal supplier, just as it is necessary for the internal supplier to continue to understand his internal customer. The supplier must know what the machinist needs and how soon he must get it to him.

▪ Reviewing Critical Relationships in Your Shop

It's a good exercise to have your employees write down the names of the people with whom they have critical relationships: employer, supervisor, customers (internal or external), and suppliers (internal or external). You should do this exercise as well. Think about each person as you write the names. Then write down what you expect of each person, and what they expect of you. Try to see yourself and your job from their viewpoints so you can understand their needs. (This will be explained in greater detail in the next chapter, Chapter Six: Areas of Success.)

This exercise will show each participant what critical relationships exist, which relationships are most important, and what areas need to improve so that all expectations are being met.

▪ Improving Your Critical Relationships

Probably the most important thing you will ever do, or ever have your people do, is to work on improving each critical relationship. This is so important, and so critical to the success of each person and the success of your company, that you cannot move your company to new levels of production or quality until everyone has completed the exercise and understands the results.

Starting with yourself, review your personal interconnection with each of your critical relationships. Try to imagine:

1. Is your connection with each of these critical relationships healthy?
2. If so, why? If not, why not?
3. What actions have you taken to improve these relationships?
4. What actions do you plan to take in the future?
5. Which of these relationships needs improving most?
6. Is there a plan you can develop for yourself that will help you improve each of your critical relationships?

If you are a top performer, these are the relationships that most interest you. If you have star performers working in your business, these are the relationships that most interest them. An expert will tell you that his critical relationships are with the people who support him, reinforce his efforts, and expect good results from him. An expert always knows who these people are, and he spends time developing a good relationship with each. That's one characteristic that makes a top performer.

When you help those who work in your machine shop understand their critical relationships, and help them nurture these relationships, you have helped your employees succeed. They can succeed because they are meeting those expectations which are truly critical to their success. Help all your employees find out for themselves what each of these critical connections want, and how to meet their expectations. When this is accomplished, your company has broken new ground. You have paved the way for true goal-setting.

Chapter Summary

- Your success is measured by what others expect of you; the same holds true for each employee.
- These significant people—your critical relations— can be grouped into four categories: employer, supervisor, customer, and supplier.
- Every employee must identify who his critical relations are, and meet their expectations in order to achieve the right results.

Chapter 6
Areas of Success

■ Areas of Success

A success area is a person's unique role as seen through the eyes of someone else with whom that person has a critical relationship. To understand a success area better, think in terms of areas of expertise. A success area, or area of expertise, is a sphere of activity someone performs that is important to one or more critical relation: supervisor, employer, customer, or supplier. A success area may be different for each critical relationship, or it may be the same for several critical relationships.

Top results are generated when each person in a company identifies his critical relationships and identifies what broad activities he must focus on to be a success from the viewpoint of those critical relationships. When the entire management team of a shop is developed enough to support each employee in his areas of success, that shop becomes a top shop. Internal problems begin to disappear, and competition among employees begins to be directed outward toward the marketplace.

■ Defining Areas of Success

One way to help employees understand what is expected of them is to help each one view his job through the eyes of each critical relation. In other words, help your employees see things from the viewpoint of these important people.

Here's an example: Let's say you have an employee who highly values his ability to produce high-quality parts. By nature, he is a craftsman. He may even judge others' abilities by how closely they can hold tolerances. He takes pride in this achievement and insists craftsmanship puts him on the "cutting edge" of what's going on.

This machinist's supervisor, however, views success in a different way. He's not the least interested in the machinist holding tolerances tighter than needed or in producing surface finishes that are considerably better than what's required. He doesn't want to see parts that should be submitted to the Smithsonian Institution for display. He has other priorities. He's interested in how quickly the machinist can machine parts that comply with the customer's requirements. He waits impatiently for the machinist to produce the next batch of quality parts. In the meantime, the machinist is trying to hit a +/- .0001 on a +/- .005 tolerance dimension with a 32 micro finish where a 125 would do!

Look at this situation from the machinist's viewpoint and from the supervisor's viewpoint. From the machinist's viewpoint, he's a success because he is producing near-perfect parts. From the supervisor's viewpoint, the machinist is a failure. He's holding up the whole schedule! If the machinist could see his performance from his supervisor's standpoint, he would understand why the supervisor nags him to do more and downgrades him on reviews.

Here's another example: Your company is machining parts that are needed desperately by the customer in order to make a shipment. The supervisor's priority is to deliver five quality parts a day, per the customer's order. It's especially important because the customer has told the supervisor that if he can receive ten parts in two days, he will renew his order with your company.

Now, one of your machinists believes he can save the company approximately $400 a month by retooling these parts. In this case, though, the supervisor isn't interested in money-saving propositions because it will delay shipping the parts and lose the renewed order. Although everyone recognizes that saving money is a noble goal, in this particular case it is not of interest to the customer who is waiting to receive his parts. And if it's not important to the supervisor or customer, it's definitely not important to the employer!

In this instance, on-time delivery is the key issue, the priority. How can the machinist succeed if he focuses on saving the company money when everyone else is interested only in on-time delivery? He can't.

Therefore, your employees must understand that to be a success in any organization, they must be successful from the viewpoints of their critical relations. A person's point of view is influenced by preconceptions and misconceptions. These preconceptions, or attitudes, are how a person thinks things should be done, how he relates to coworkers, and what he dreams of becoming. Personal attitudes are important to everyone, of course, because they are the motivating force behind our actions. They are the "how and why" of work. But to succeed, you and your employees cannot allow yourselves to be biased by your personal values. The requirements a person sets for himself may conflict with the actual requirements of the job as determined by his critical relationships. Sometimes a machinist may have to give up a success area he *thinks* is important for one his supervisor *insists* is more important.

Certainly, a person has to feel good about what he does, and what he's accomplished. But first he must meet others' expectations. Job satisfaction should come from meeting *others'* needs.

▪ Help Your Employees Establish Success Areas

Each person must decide what the success areas are for his job. No one can really do this for another person. An employer or supervisor can make a suggestion, and the suggestion should be welcomed by the machinist, but the thinking a machinist does that goes into defining a success area is as important as the success area itself! When a person makes his own decisions about critical relationships, that person takes ownership of the idea, and it becomes clearer and means more to him than if it is given to him by someone else.

Each employee—including you—should begin by reviewing his list of critical relationships and the general expectations associated with each (Chapter Five: Critical Relationships). Using this as a base, have each employee make a list of specific areas of success connected with each critical relationship. Some suggested success areas to consider are sales, speed, accuracy, cost cutting, increased production, and product development. Have your employees review their lists frequently, and add or subtract success areas when needed.

For example, encourage each machinist to look at what he is doing through his employer's eyes. Ask him: Are you helping the company make a profit? Look at what you are doing through your supervisor's eyes. Are you doing what he expects? Are you producing the work he wants in the quickest and most efficient way? If you were your own supervisor, what would you say about your work? From the customer's viewpoint, are you giving him exactly what he ordered? Will he get it on time? From the supplier's viewpoint, are you clearly communicating your supply needs?

Each person must nurture these critical relationships and see them as partnerships. Pay attention to what each of these people say and what they imply. Learn what's important to them. Then fulfill their expectations. This is what everyone is paid to do—to produce the results expected in these relationships.

Ask each employee to go through this exercise from the viewpoint of each critical relationship. Asking these questions gives each employee an entirely different slant on what he should be doing, and how he should be doing it. Let's review the thought process in more detail to help you understand what everyone in your shop must do to be successful.

What the Owner Expects

The owner's main interest is that his company makes a profit. He may also be interested in cutting costs and exploring ideas for the company's future development. An owner wants each employee to earn his salary. An owner asks himself:

1. Am I making a profit?
2. Are costs being contained?
3. Is the company's mission being fulfilled?

These three major questions are on every owner's mind. These are areas the employer is directly responsible for, which is why they are important. With these priorities in mind, each employee should ask himself:

1. What am I doing to help the owner make a profit?
2. How am I containing costs?
3. How can I help the future development of this company?

The success areas related to the employer's viewpoint will differ from department to department and person to person within a shop. These can be difficult questions for an employee to answer because people don't usually think about these things. Yet the answers to these questions are critical to all employees' success. That's why it takes careful thought for each employee to answer each of the above questions as truthfully as possible, so success areas can be accurately identified. A machinist might answer these questions this way:

- Increase productivity (profit)
- Care for equipment (costs)
- Work within a budget (costs)

When the machinist knows what he must do to succeed through the employer's eyes—how to meet the employer's expectations—he can figure out the actions he must take.

You must help your employees recognize that success areas translate into specific actions. For example, let's say your company is awarded a large contract. To be competitive, you've had to shorten the production schedule. The employer is expecting everyone to be working full time, with no days off. The foreman may even put on a second shift so the schedule can be met.

From the viewpoint of the machinist, then, one of his areas of success would be perfect attendance. He knows his employer expects him to work every day, at least until the contract is completed, so that the company improves its chances of making a profit by meeting the contract obligations.

What a Supervisor Expects

A supervisor's main focus is getting those whom he supervises to do more work so he can give them more work to do. He wants everyone to work quickly and accurately. A supervisor is always thinking:

1. Can he work faster?
2. Can he do more work if I give him more work to do?
3. Can he produce better quality?

Therefore, for a machinist to understand what he must do from his supervisor's viewpoint, he must find answers to the questions that are foremost in his supervisor's mind.

1. How can I increase efficiency?
2. What additional work can I do?
3. What can I do to ensure quality in my work?

The following are some of the machinist's possible success areas:

- Produce quality work (quality)
- Get the job done quickly (speed)
- Do additional work (profit)
- Make fewer mistakes (profit and quality)

A machinist's answers to these questions are vital to his success because his supervisor is the most influential person at work. His supervisor can hire or fire him, or make his life happy or miserable. Supervisors can report good work to others—to the owner, fellow workers, the customer, and everyone else whose opinion matters. Through the supervisor, an employee's work gets approved and passed on to others.

What the Customer Expects

The customer is basically interested in quality, competitive pricing, and on-time deliveries. The customer asks himself:

1. How good is it?
2. How much does it cost?
3. How fast can I get it?

At the root of every successful company is excellent customer service. For a company to succeed in a highly competitive field, all those in the company must enthusiastically share the viewpoint of the customer. When everyone in the company knows what the customer wants and expects, each person can identify at least one success area to which he can contribute.

To help define how to succeed from the viewpoint of a customer, each employee must answer these questions:

1. How can I make a more consistent quality product for the customer?
2. What can I do to reduce the cost of manufacturing, and thereby reduce the cost to the customer?
3. What can I do to get this product to him on time?

A shop cannot fail if each employee embraces the customers' concerns and takes action. In a large corporation a machinist may be removed from the actual customer. For instance, if your company builds airplane parts, the machinist has nothing directly to do with the overall cost or delivery time of the final product, the airplane. However, knowing what the customer expects makes him a better performer. He may have ideas about developing the quality of his specific task or ways of increasing efficiency that may affect the outcome of the entire production process.

When answering the above questions, an employee begins to identify those areas of activity that bring him success from his customer's viewpoint. Some of the answers to the questions may be:

- Pay greater attention to detail (quality)
- Produce less scrap (cost)
- Work more closely with estimating and production (speed)
- Ensure timeliness of delivery (speed)
- Respond quickly to customer questions (quality)
- Review specifications (cost and quality)

Customer service is not strictly up to the salespeople. The customers' needs and expectations can be met, at least in part, by all employees.

What Your Supplier Expects

Your supplier wants to know exactly what your shop needs so it can do its job. Your supplier is mostly interested in receiving the order in time so he can fill it promptly. And he wants to supply the right items. Your supplier wants to know:

1. Did I get accurate specifications for the order?
2. Do I have enough time to ship it?
3. Are my costs competitive?

To succeed in the supplier's eyes, you or perhaps the purchasing clerk must ask the following:

1. How can I make sure I order precisely what we need?
2. How much advance time does my supplier need to fill the order?
3. Should I give my supplier feedback? (For example, can I get this item cheaper somewhere else?)

The answers to these questions help your shop succeed from the suppliers' viewpoints. Your shop's success areas in relation to your supplier may be:

- Place orders in advance (timeliness)
- Order accurately (correct delivery)
- Let the supplier know how he's doing (feedback)

There is nothing more frustrating than receiving the wrong materials, the wrong tools, or an incomplete piece of equipment. Although most suppliers run their business by giving their customers what they want, mistakes are made. However, sometimes the mistake isn't the supplier's. Your careful attention to your supplier's needs will prevent mistakes and delays.

Giving Feedback to Suppliers

It is expensive for the shop, the supplier, and therefore your customer when a vendor delivery is late or the product is inadequate. And although these costly mistakes may make you want to change suppliers, it's often far wiser to work with the supplier to solve delivery problems and establish a good working relationship, than to skip from supplier to supplier, always looking for the lowest price or quickest delivery.

The best way to accomplish this is by offering feedback. Every supplier appreciates a call from a customer. Tell him how he's doing, where the problem areas are, and what you'd like to see change. If you're unhappy with a price increase, call

(cont.)

■ **Giving Feedback to Suppliers...** *(continued)*
your supplier and talk with him about it. Give the supplier information he can use to make his service better.

For example, suppose you have an established account with a supplier you've been with for years, but find you can get the same tools, materials, or service from the supplier's competitor for 5% less. The best thing to do is to call your regular vendor and talk about the price difference. If you've worked for years to establish a good relationship with your supplier and can depend upon him to come through for you, you may ultimately decide that the 5% isn't important enough to force you to change vendors. But both you and your vendor will benefit from this discussion.

Let's review the case of a machinist running a CNC machining center. Another machinist who works in the tooling department is one of the CNC machinist's suppliers because he provides the tools and tooling needed to do the job. It's important for these two to nurture their relationship so they can both do their jobs successfully. By improving their relationship, they can solve such common problems as identifying the tools needed to do a job and the amount of time required to prepare the tool.

For example, as they work to improve their relationship, they will communicate to each other the project requirements at a job's early stage. The machinist in the tooling department will always be given enough time to make the tools required by the CNC machinist, and the CNC operator will know he'll receive the tools on time.

■ Seeing Eye to Eye

Remind your employees not to jump to conclusions about what is expected in any of these relationships. If the priorities of the employer or supervisor, for example, appear to conflict with the machinist, or if someone doesn't understand what the employer or supervisor has in mind, communicate through frank discussion. Resolve the discrepancy. It is absolutely mandatory that both people in the relationship agree on the specific success areas for the relationship. Otherwise, no one can be satisfied or successful. And if an employee cannot succeed in what he was hired to do, the whole shop fails.

Your employees can communicate their expectations to one another by filling out Expectation Charts and discussing the results. Every employee should have at least two: one that defines expectations between himself and his supervisor, and one that defines expectations between himself and the person down the line. Note that both people in the relationship are given an opportunity to express their expectations of each other.

EXPECTATION CHART

SUPPLIER	CUSTOMER/RECEIVER
Name: Position:	Name: Position:
List Expectations	List Expectations

When filling out Expectation Charts, your employees should keep these two thoughts in mind:

1. Don't include more than three of four expectations on the chart, otherwise it becomes a list of complaints. Think of how different an employee would feel if even one or two of his expectations were acted upon. It would change his whole attitude at work! Therefore, the number of expectations an employee has is not what's important, so he shouldn't worry if he has only a few.

2. Keep each expectation on the list short and focused. Complete sentences aren't necessary; phrases are enough to express an expectation. What is important is that the Expectation Chart begins the process of communication between employees in critical relationships.

Remind employees that not all expectations have immediate solutions. Expectations take time to fulfill, so they shouldn't expect immediate results.

CASE STUDY	Jerry Knolls, a supervisor at Vault Machine Works, described the four critical relations in business to all employees at a company meeting. He

explained that the purpose was to increase communication and improve relationships between workers, which would lead to increased production. Jerry gave each employee at Vault Machine Works a stack of Expectation Charts and showed them how to fill them out.

Jason Witcomb is a machinist at Vault. He completed the right side of his first Expectation Chart by writing down his expectations of his direct supervisor, Jerry Knolls.

EXPECTATION CHART

SUPPLIER	CUSTOMER/RECEIVER
Name: Jerry Knolls **Position:** Supervisor	**Name:** Jason Witcomb **Position:** Machinist
List Expectations	**List Expectations**
More work done	Fair treatment- not forced to perform to unreasonable levels.
Quality work	Provided quality tools and equipment - not expected to use dull or improper cutters or use equipment that is incapable of holding the required tolerances.
Attendance - at work on time	Provide a clean and adequately lit place to work in.
Work done efficiently	Feedback on how I'm doing. Open to my ideas. Training and direction for improvement. Rewards for excellence.

Then Jason gave the chart to his supervisor, Jerry. When Jerry discussed Jason's Expectation Chart with him, Jerry told Jason to increase his output of work. Jason promptly noted this information on the upper-left side of his Expectation Chart—More work done. He also noted the other expectations his supervisor had for him.

(cont.)

Jerry also suggested they meet for a short time once a week to review each others' expectations. Jason and Jerry then set about to improve this relationship by fulfilling each others' expectations. For example, Jason explained to Jerry that frequently he was unable to locate the proper cutting tools to do a job and was forced to use dull ones. Jerry subsequently set up procedures to insure that there were always sharp cutting tools available.

Sharon, another Vault employee, operates a stretch form machine and receives most of her work from Jason. This relationship is critical because sloppy or incomplete work on Jason's part only makes more work for Sharon. When Sharon receives poor work she becomes unhappy and angry.

Sharon identified Jason as one of her critical relations and filled out the right side of her own Expectation Chart. Jason then added his expectations of her to the left side. At the same time, he received what he needed from them in order to be successful.

EXPECTATION CHART

SUPPLIER	CUSTOMER/RECEIVER
Name: Jason	**Name:** Sharon
Position: Machinist	**Position:** Machinist
List Expectations	**List Expectations**
Feedback on performance	Parts clean and deburred
Discuss with me first if there's a problem with my production	Accurate parts count
	Discrepant parts properly tagged

When Jason identified and understood who his critical relations were, he immediately began to understand what each relationship required. Then he began to improve his relationships with Jerry and Sharon by meeting their expectations.

If an employee refuses to cooperate with this system, even after these important steps have been taken, he can bring the whole production to a standstill. At this point, the manager must step in and carefully explain to him what he is doing so that he understands. He must be told that his refusal to change jeopardizes his job and the success of the company. If he still refuses to identify the proper success areas and take the actions required by his critical relations, he must be removed from the production cycle.

The permanent solution, of course, is to create an environment in the workplace where identifying and improving critical relationships is the norm, and employees actively seek out success areas and agree upon them because that's what they are—the only area of operation in which you can have success.

Chapter Summary

- A success area is an activity that a worker performs that is important to one of his critical relations.
- Based on critical relations, every employee must identify which activities, or success areas, are important.
- Both people in a critical relationship must agree on the success areas. An Expectation Chart is a good tool for beginning a discussion of mutual expectations.

Chapter 7
Using Success Areas to Set Goals

■ Why Set Goals?

Imagine your favorite sport. You enjoy it, at least in part, because there is some system of scorekeeping that tells you how well your team is doing compared to its prior performances and the current performance of the other team. When you know the score, two things happen:

1. Performance improves because the winning team wants to maintain its lead, and the losing team is motivated to pull ahead.
2. The activity becomes more enjoyable for everyone.

Imagine how boring a sport would be if no one knew the score of a game until days or weeks after the game was over! Fans would stop attending the game!

In the same way, every employee must know the rules of the game (identify success areas) in order to figure out how to win the game (set goals) and be successful. When success areas are used to set individual and overall shop goals, all employees can accurately measure their progress toward achieving the results you, and their other critical relations, are expecting. A goal is a target, an *immediate performance indicator*. With goals, employees begin to see the importance of each task they perform, how it fits into the "big picture," and they start to realize that everyone in the shop is moving in the same direction. The probability that you and your employees will achieve full potential is greatly enhanced when everyone knows their "performance score."

A shop manager should review all employees' goals, and may even record data points and trend lines as each employee measures his progress. Management must help employees achieve goals. When a person doesn't achieve a goal, or cannot achieve a goal, go back to the drawing board. Maybe there is not enough reinforcement. Maybe some sort of barrier exists. Or maybe the goal is not realistic or appropriate, and should be altered.

Some people dislike goals because they don't want to be "goal driven," or have their work judged by whether they attain a certain performance level. They may feel they will get criticized, or even fired, if they don't meet certain goals. But these are merely excuses. All employees must set personal goals in order to chart their progress toward results. Goals let individuals know they're on the right track because they don't have to "second-guess" the supervisor or another department.

■ When to Set Goals

Before individuals can set goals that effectively work for them, the corporate culture must change. Everyone has to feel the company is on the verge of new growth. There must be a sense of the corporate mission. Critical relationships and success areas must be defined, and out of these relationships, goals must be identified. Individuals can then work their way up to the expert level. Above all, the company's management must set an example of leadership, and good behavior and good results must be reinforced and rewarded. These are the steps you've been following, and will continue to pursue, as you work through this book.

Many companies make the mistake of having individuals set goals too early, before the basics are set in place. When personal goals are set before the corporate "homework" is done, two things happen:

1. The goals go nowhere. Everyone soon loses interest in setting goals because the goals don't seem to relate to what the company is doing. Soon the goal-setting process is viewed as a failure.

2. People view the goals as something else they have to do—
another task. They view it this way because they had no part
in the goal-setting process, therefore the goals have no value
or meaning. The employees may even become suspicious.
Will the company become goal-driven? Will people lose their
jobs if goals aren't met?

Focus on success, then set goals. It's a mistake to set goals first.
If your shop is not experiencing success right now—if production
is at a standstill—setting goals first won't work. In fact, setting
goals can create additional pressure because even if goals are
met, nothing happens. In the final result, goals do not turn a
company around. *People* turn a company around. But goals will
aid your employees in moving forward as long as the preliminary
groundwork has been laid.

▪ Arriving at Goals

Setting the right goals is simplified when you and your employees use the information at hand. Review your own list of critical
relationships and the corresponding success areas. Then, set one
goal that accurately defines an activity for each success area. Have
each of your employees do the same for their success areas. The
thought process looks like this:

Critical Relationship > Success Area > Goal

Keep in mind that each goal must be observable and measurable. This is the only way a goal setter will know he is improving
his performance. Therefore, begin each goal with a symbol that
represents a number, dollar amount, percent, or ratio, such as #,
$, %, or /. The second component of each goal relates to a spe-
cific task. Every task must be linked to a success area as determined by critical relationships.

Some examples of goals include:

% of defects compared to total production

# of quality items produced

# of rejections

# of defects

$ spent on training

produced per hour

of orders delivered on time

% of labor hours compared to actual hours

# of complaints

# of orders sold

$ sold

$ costs cut

Once you and your employees have reached this point, the symbols can be replaced with actual figures, such as **0 defects** or **5 quality parts per day**. This number becomes the standard to which actual performance is compared. It is the "score." (The numerical value of goals will be discussed in greater detail in Chapter Eight: Tracking Goal Progress.)

Your shop will have overall goals, and each individual will have personal goals. Your employees should work with you in setting their own goals to ensure that they are correct and meet the needs of their critical relations. By the same token, you should work with your employees in setting the shop's overall goals so that your employees have a personal stake in meeting the overall goals.

CASE STUDY   Mo Everson is in charge of scheduling at MJ Precision Machining. As sometimes happens in small shops, Mo promised project completion dates he could not keep, just to get work into the shop. His scheduling often conflicted with the production foreman. This caused considerable frustration. In a short time, Mo's promises of quick completion dates backfired; customers became angry and contracts were lost when these completion dates failed to be met.

Mo sat down with the shop owner and the production foreman to discuss the matter. They agreed that whatever the cost, even losing a contract, they would revise their scheduling so

(cont.)

that each customer received an accurate ship date. There would be no more panic to meet an impossible schedule.

Therefore, Mo and the shop owner agreed that a success area for Mo (and therefore the company!) was accurate ship dates. From this, Mo devised this goal for himself:

# of jobs completed on time per month / # of jobs promised

In other words, Mo is going to find the ratio between the number of jobs completed and the number promised. He is aiming for a 100% ratio.

Let's study the characteristics of Mo's goal:

1. It is measurable. Mo knows how he is doing by looking at the numbers: **# of jobs completed on time in relation to # of jobs promised**. If he completes 11 jobs during the month on time, and promised 12, he has a ratio of 11/12, or a 91.6% on-time completion rate.
2. It's what Mo, his supervisor, and the production department agree is important to achieve.
3. The more accurate the schedule—the closer Mo gets to 100%—the more success Mo feels.

Consider other goals Mo could have defined for himself, and whether they are measurable enough for Mo to use to chart his progress toward success.

# of labor hours quoted / # labor hours spent to complete the job
$ saved through scrap reduction
# of items returned for rework

Each of these goals is measurable, and can either be decreased or increased, depending upon what Mo's critical relations define as success. By setting this goal for himself, Mo slowly but steadily helped his machine shop regain its reputation as a business that gave reliable product ship dates.

▪ What to Consider When Setting Goals

Each goal must be directly related to a success area, and each success area must be crucial to a critical relationship. If a person sets too many goals, he is probably trying to do someone else's job. He should limit his goals, and focus on only those things that are crucial to his own job.

To help each person identify what is crucial to his job, have each person answer these questions:

1. When was the last time someone was proud of my work? What did I do to earn that praise? For example, a supervisor recently came up to a machinist and said, "I really liked how quickly you machined that last order." The machinist's success area—from the supervisor's viewpoint—is speed. His goal could be **# of parts machined within the scheduled time.**

2. When was the last time I was proud of my work? At the end of the day, what would I brag to my spouse about regarding my work performance? Usually you are proud of what you did at work because what you did was a success for the whole company; it had far-reaching ramifications. Therefore, it may be a goal.

3. What would I tell my replacement about my job while I went on vacation? Most likely, what someone would explain to his replacement are the most important things about his job. For instance, the tooling supervisor might tell his replacement, "Be sure to keep this schedule up-to-date." Thus, meeting deadlines is one of that supervisor's goals.

4. If I owned the company I work for, what would be the one result I would expect from the job I do? Look at things from the owner's point of view.

5. If my employer said I'd earn 50% of any profits I contributed to the company, what part of my job would I focus on?

6. What would make my customers happy? As the manager, make a list of items that make your shop's customers satisfied, for example, responding quickly to a customer's telephone call (**# of minutes between customer call and response**), or information for your customer that their order is ahead of schedule (**# of days ahead of schedule/actual schedule**).

7. What would cause my customers to get angry or cancel an order? This information gives you clues as to what your shop must do to be a success from your customers' viewpoint.

8. What could happen in my job that would be so bad that I'd get fired for it?

9. If an incompetent person were doing my job, what's the first thing that would go wrong?
10. If my job were eliminated, what would go wrong with the company?
11. What are the major problems I handle when I do my job?

These questions help each person, especially you, focus on the viewpoints of critical relations. They help everyone identify what they do and see how crucial it is to the company. Each question defines an area of success and the specific tasks related to it. Each of these tasks should have a specific, measurable goal associated with it.

▪ The Five Goal Tests

When you and your employees are setting goals for yourselves, apply the following five tests to each one. If the goal passes all of these tests, then it is an appropriate, attainable goal.

Test # 1: The Mission Test

Relate the goal to your company's mission. Is this goal directly supportive of your company's mission? If not, get rid of it.

Test # 2: The Balance Test

A goal must not throw other departments or other individuals dependent upon the goal setter's output out of balance. Ask, "Does this goal establish a greater balance between departments?"

A goal is balanced if "overperformance" would not have an adverse impact on the company. For example, if a salesperson's goal is **$ value booked**, his overperformance could be a problem if the orders he takes (or the delivery dates he promises) are unrealistic and put an impossible burden on other departments that would force them to get behind in the schedule. The shop's capabilities must be in line with the salesperson's sales goal. A goal fails when it is not profitable for the company, or when it throws other departments out of kilter.

If you sense an imbalance in a goal, the goal setter must redefine it or add another component to even it out. For example, **$ value booked** could be clarified as **$ value booked / $ shipped**

per month. Or a better work load indicator might be stated as **labor hours booked / labor hours completed**. Or it could be divided into two goals: **# labor hours booked** and **$ profitability on each order**.

Test # 3: The Uniqueness Test

Make certain each goal is unique to the goal setter. The goal setter must ask himself, "Is my goal unique to me (or to the job I am doing)? Is it what *I* must do to succeed at my job? Does anyone else have more control over this task than I do?" If the answer is yes, then the goal belongs to another person or department in the company.

The one exception is this: if one person's job description is identical to that of someone else, then they may have identical goals.

Test # 4: The Push-down Test

Management must always be pushed to the lowest level. In other words, if a subordinate can do the job you are doing, or has greater influence over the job than you do, *let him do it!*

As an example, you may consider it your job to make certain all quotes are submitted on time, so your success goal might be **# of quotes submitted on time.** However, if your shop's contracts administrator or assistant is the one who gathers the data (labor hours, material prices, outside processing costs, etc.) and compiles the quotes, **# of quotes submitted on time** should be that person's goal, not yours.

A successful business constantly pushes management downward until the responsibility for getting the job done has reached the person who has the most control over getting the job done. Make certain all goals have been pushed down to the lowest correct levels.

Test # 5: The 80% Test

Apply the 80% test in this way:

1. Each of the goals is 80% under the goal setter's control.
2. All of one person's goals together represent 80% of what that person does at work.

Many of your responsibilities (and everyone else's) will never be covered by goals. They are important parts of your work, such as making telephone calls, putting your office or workstation in order, and meeting with other departments, but they are not in the 80% category of your unique responsibilities.

Typically, a machinist will have at least one goal related to the employer's needs, at least one related to the supervisor's viewpoint, and one related to the person who receives his work (his customer). He may also set one or two goals strictly for himself.

| **CASE STUDY** | At Twin City Machining, Inc., Matthew Thomas's main job is to purchase materials and tools for the shop. Matthew has identified the shop fore- |

man as one of his critical relationships—his customer. It is important for Matthew to succeed in providing materials on time because the foreman relies heavily on him to get the materials to the shop floor when he needs them. Matthew set a goal for himself to order and receive materials and tools in a timely manner.

He completed a company Goal Test form, as shown below, to make certain his goal was in line.

GOAL TEST FORM TWIN CITY MACHINING, INC.		
Name: Matthew Thomas	**Goal:** To order and receive material and tools in a timely manner.	
MISSION TEST		
How is your goal directly supportive of the company's mission of QUALITY, SERVICE and PRICE		
My goal directly supports our mission of providing quality service to our customers. If the shop receives materials and tools on schedule they are then better able to maintain their production schedule and provide the customer with on-time deliveries.		
BALANCE TEST		
Please identify all departments or individuals that may be negatively affected by you achieving your goal. List any impact on them.		
DEPT/PERSON	**IMPACT**	
NONE		
UNIQUENESS TEST		
Please explain why you must achieve this goal in order to succeed at your job.		
The shop relies heavily on material and tools being available when they need them. If I fail at my job then the company fails its mission.		
PUSH-DOWN TEST / 80% CONTROL TEST		
Identify each department or person who may have some effect or control of your goal. List what issues may be involved. Enter your "best guess" percent of control that department or person might have.		
DEPT/PERSON	**ISSUE**	**% CONTROL**
Planning Dept	Timely identification of required materials and tools.	10%

After completing the Goal Test Form, Matthew determined that his goal was attainable. It also gave him a clearer picture of how much of his goal was under his control, and who else affected his ability to reach his goal.

▪ Two Types of Goal Setting

It is better to aim for perfection and miss, than to aim for imperfection and hit your mark.

There are two types of goal setting:

1. Individual—a goal set by oneself
2. Participative—a goal set in conjunction with others

Setting goals is just one step on the way to getting your company on track and forming effective teams. Therefore, you will set some goals for yourself (individual), and you will set other goals after discussing them with others (participative). Likewise, your employees will set some individual and some participative goals for themselves. At first, more people will be more comfortable using the individual goal-setting method. But, as your employees gain confidence in their future, individuals will more frequently set effective goals after consulting with others. Building a strong foundation for teams, individuals will increasingly engage in participative goal setting, relying especially on those with whom they will be working as a team.

▪ Importance of Setting Individual Goals

No one can set an effective goal for another person. A goal is a *personal* target for success, so a person must set his own goals. He must have his own reason for setting the goal, and develop his own ideas of how to achieve it. He must have a personal commitment to the goal, an investment of his own time in identifying it, and an obligation to himself to honor it.

There are exceptions, of course. When many individuals in a company perform the same tasks, they may have the same goals. However, each person must do his own thinking and arrive at the goals, similar though they may be, otherwise the goals will have little value.

Sometimes you may not wish to discuss your goals with others. For example, if goal setting is not yet commonplace in your company, you may want your goal setting to remain a personal activity for now. Or, you may have a personal goal that you're just not interested in sharing with others. Don't feel compelled to share any or all of your personal goals, and don't force your employees to share all of their goals either.

■ Setting Goals in Participation with Others

The main problem in individually setting goals is that the goals may not be in perspective. It's difficult for any individual, even the company's top person, to always have a clear vision of what the company is doing and where it's going at any given time. A goal setter gets a clearer picture after discussion with others. This is participative goal setting.

Anyone can accomplish participative goal setting in one of three ways:

1. Set goals after discussion with those who work for or with the goal setter. For example, as a manager, you can ask your machinists what their set-up efficiency goals are for the future. Or ask them what their scrap rate goals are for the next six months. Tell them of a tentative goal, and ask them for feedback. This gives you a broader picture of how things are developing in one of your departments or in your company, and what to expect. When you have this information, your final goals will be clearer because you will understand how your goals pertain to those around you.

2. Set goals individually, but involve other employees in brainstorming on how to achieve it. For example, a salesperson may decide to confirm six major contracts in the next six months. He's not sure the company can tool up for this new work, and he wants his personal goal to be supported by the shop's capacity. So, he should work with his coworkers on preparing for an increased workload before he starts bringing in the new business.

3. Ask someone to set a goal on behalf of the goal setter. This can be an important decision on the goal setter's part. For example, if you are the company's owner, you might ask

one of your shop's professionals or experts—your foreman or a supervisor, or even a machinist you trust—what you expect to achieve, and ask him to set or suggest a goal for you. By doing this, you build trust between you and the individual, you add to that person's confidence, and you demonstrate your willingness to be a team player. However, if one person asks someone else to set a goal—not merely suggest one—for him, he must accept it.

If coworkers disagree with one person's goals, ask them why. Use their feedback to re-evaluate the goals. Either the goal setter is on the wrong track and needs to adjust his goals, or the co-workers are not looking at the big picture and need to be shown why the goals are correct. In either case, goals will be more accurate and better defined thanks to others' input.

CASE STUDY   Vince Miller works for JHS Manufacturing, a company outside Oakland, California, that manufactures anchors for a large marine supply company.

JHS received an order for 850 30-lb. anchors, to be delivered before the opening of boating season. Vince was assigned to drill fitting holes in both sides of each anchor. Vince reviewed the job and set his goals:

Critical Relationship: MaryAnn Bacon, Supervisor
Project: Work Order X-37337-92, Davis Marine Supply,
        Drill fitting holes.
Success Area: Quality
Goals: # of anchors finished

When Vince felt he had properly identified his goal, he showed it to his supervisor, MaryAnn. Vince explained to her how he arrived at his goal.

MaryAnn said, "The anchor castings are on a pallet. You'll have to lift each 30 lb. anchor to the drill press table, drill the fitting hole, lift the anchor to turn it over, and drill the other fitting hole. Then you'll have to return the finished anchor to the pallet and lift another anchor into place. This is heavy work."

Vince mentioned that he was strong, and saw no problem with the lifting.

(cont.)

MaryAnn then reminded Vince that boating season begins May 4th, and the 850 anchors had to be finished before then. In fact, they should ship the first 100 anchors as soon as they were ready.

"I think speed is more important than quality in this case," MaryAnn said.

Vince agreed to change his success area from Quality to Speed. Then Vince suggested that he measure for accuracy instead of speed, and MaryAnn agreed. Vince said, "If I measure # of fittings drilled rather than # of anchors finished, I'll get a more accurate picture of how well I'm doing."

"You might want to add another goal, such as # of errors," MaryAnn suggested. "A perfect score would be 1700 fitting holes drilled with no errors. But remember, speed is what counts. We've got to get these finished anchors to Davis Marine before the first of May."

Vince changed his goal to the following:

Critical Relationship: MaryAnn Bacon, Supervisor
Project: Work Order X-37337-92, Davis Marine Supply, Drill
       fitting holes.
Success Area: Speed
Goals: # of fitting holes drilled
       # of errors

Vince told MaryAnn that he would be able to drill 20 fitting holes to complete 10 anchors a day. MaryAnn said she would be happy to see 15 completed anchors, each accurately drilled.

Vince suggested that if JHS purchased two hydraulic pallet jacks, one for each end of the drill press table, he could easily increase his output, and that it would not be difficult to meet the schedule. These jacks would be used to raise or lower the parts to the table height, thereby eliminating the need to bend over and pick the parts up or put them on the finished parts pallet.

MaryAnn agreed and immediately purchased the hydraulic jacks. The operation was a success.

■ Benefits of Participative Goal Setting

Participative goal setting offers many benefits:

1. It encourages commitment rather than compliance. When two people have agreed to a goal, they both have a personal investment in achieving it.

2. It encourages creativity. Those closest to the problem often know best what is truly possible to accomplish, and how best to achieve it.

3. It encourages company loyalty. The more employees are encouraged to discuss goal setting and problem solving with upper management, the more they tend to think in terms of "the good of the company."

4. The best thinking—the most information and ideas—can come from all concerned.

5. Continuous discussion and review of goals allows people to accept changes when there is a shift in the original forecast. People resent changing goals if they had no input in setting the goals in the first place.

6. Participative goal setting provides an objective basis for review and feedback. People won't take review personally.

7. It encourages teamwork.

8. Goal setting by negotiation helps manage conflict by breaking down complex operations into components.

9. It provides a common language between worker and manager, and between coworkers.

10. Participative goal setting is a common corporate mission that bonds people. It helps get everyone focused in the same direction.

■ Questions and Answers About Goal Setting

The following are some common questions your employees may ask about goal setting. Here are the answers you can give them:

Questions	Answers
How long do I keep a goal?	You don't keep it forever. Keep a goal until it is not an issue with you. Then drop it or modify it.
How many goals does a person need?	Eight to ten is about right. Thirty is too many. If you have thirty, you are taking too much responsibility for others' work.

Questions	Answers
When is a goal no longer an issue?	When one of your critical relations announces a change in priorities, or when a new person comes into your position because you are promoted, your goal should no longer be an issue.
Should I and my supervisor have similar goals?	You and your supervisor should agree on your goals, but they must be unique to you. If your goal is the same as someone else's, you might not need it. You may be spending too much time on detail, or you may be trying to do someone else's job. The only time your goal should be identical to someone else's is when you're both doing identical work.
Can I get rid of or delegate a goal?	A goal must be critical to your success. If it is not critical to you, it should not be one of your goals. Always try to push a goal down to a lower level. For example, if you have a goal that says **# of hours setting up a job compared to established setup standards** because it's your job to make certain short setup times occur, but you don't actually do the setup, this goal belongs to the person who does the setups. More accurately, your goal might be **% setup efficiency per month**. That goal would allow you to measure your success rate and devise schemes for shortening the monthly setup times. _(cont.)_

Questions	Answers
My goal reflects exactly what I oversee, is that correct?	Yes. Ask yourself, "What do I do and how can I measure it? How will I know that I succeeded?"
Are there standard goals that I can adopt?	Yes. Some activities have standard goals. However, you should think through your goals yourself. Find the ones that are important to you—that describe exactly what you must do to succeed in the eyes of your critical relations.
Is it true that if I have the most control over a function, then it should have a corresponding goal?	Yes. Set at least one goal based on that function.

Chapter Summary

- Success areas can be broken down into specific goals that will show employees how well they are meeting others' expectations.
- A goal has two components—a numeric measure and an action—and must be observable and measurable.
- A person can set goals by himself (individual goal setting) or in conjunction with others (participative goal setting).

Chapter 8
Tracking Goal Progress

■ Three-level Goals

For best results, break goals down into three numerical levels. Three-level goals offer a greater feeling of control by allowing the goal setter to work progressively toward the highest levels of achievement. Arriving at the numerical values for three-level goals can seem difficult at first, but such goals are more realistic indicators of progress than single-level goals. Once you understand the math that's involved, you and your employees will become adept at setting three-level goals.

The three levels are:

1. Minimum. This level is a person's threshold of allowable performance. If he performs below this level, he has a problem. A "minimum" level reflects a goal of trying to reduce something, such as **# of errors**, or of increasing something, such as **# of quality items produced**.

2. Satisfactory. A person's satisfactory level is his next achievable level of performance.

3. Outstanding. This is the most important level of excellence. When a worker hits his outstanding level, he breaks new ground.

▪ Establishing the Right Levels

There are two methods of establishing the numerical value of a goal: intuitive and statistical. Both are equally valid. After setting his goal type, individual or participative, a person must decide whether he is going to use the intuitive or statistical method to arrive at the right numbers. The important thing is not the method a person uses to set his goals, but whether he increases his performance in his own eyes and from the viewpoints of his critical relations.

How to Set an Intuitive Three-level Goal

To set an intuitive three-level goal, gather statistics on a task for several weeks (or longer, if possible). The more information a person gathers, the more accurately it reflects his current level of activity.

Take time to gather this information. Set a date, such as a month or so in advance, by which time all the information will be collected. This gives a person time to do the necessary record-keeping so he has all the right information required.

After information for each goal is collected, it can be converted into three-level goals. Here's how to set a three-level goal using the intuitive method and the collected information.

First, take the information gathered for one task. Next, calculate the average level of activity by adding the data points and dividing by the total number of data points. After a person has the average, have him find his highest and lowest levels of performance from his list of data points.

To set a minimum goal level, select the number halfway between the average and worst performance. To set a satisfactory goal level, select the number halfway between the average and best performance.

Setting an outstanding goal level is an individual choice—it's whatever the person thinks he can eventually do. In choosing this level, consider the requirements of the job, the expectations the person has for himself, and the company's long-range plans.

Here's an example of collecting data to set an intuitive goal. David, a drill-press operator, is told by Joanne, the shop foreman, that she wants to see at least 150 parts per day with a less than 1%

defect rate. David wants to test these numbers, and set his own realistic goal. The 5" stainless steel cylinder David cuts and drills is expensive material, so waste is a consideration. Also, any out-of-tolerance condition might not be noticed until days after the parts are cut and drilled, which means other machinists on subsequent operations must alter their schedule to accommodate the error.

David identified the following formulas for success, and collected this data:

Critical Relationship	Success Area	Goal	Data	
Shop foreman	Quantity	# of parts produced per day	Day	Qty
			Monday	145
			Tuesday	150
			Wednesday	140
			Thursday	160
			Friday	155

Critical Relationship	Success Area	Goal	Data	
Shop foreman	Defect free parts	# of defects per day	Day	Qty
			Wednesday	2
			Thursday	1

In one week, Monday through Friday, David produced 750 cylinders. Three were returned with defects, although these defective parts were not actually produced on the day they were returned to David.

David calculated that he could average cutting and drilling 150 cylinders a day, with an error rate of 3/5 per day, which he rounded off to 1 per day. His highest achievement was 160 per day, and his lowest achievement for the week was 140. His highest number of defects was 2, and his lowest was 0.

Therefore, David set his intuitive goals as follows:

of parts produced each day

minimum	satisfactory	outstanding
145	155	165

David continued figuring and arrived at these goals. The minimum goal, 145, is halfway between his average performance (150) and his lowest performance (140). His satisfactory goal, 155, is halfway between his average (150) and his highest performance (160). His outstanding goal is his choice. David chose 165 because he felt that without interruptions he could produce 165 parts.

Next, using the same formula for setting intuitive goals, David set his goal for defects:

of defects per day

minimum	satisfactory	outstanding
2	1	0

How to Set a Statistical Three-level Goal

Setting a statistical three-level goal requires a more complex procedure. To set a statistical goal, gather information on performance for at least one business quarter. The more data gathered, the more accurate the statistical goal will be. After quarterly results have been gathered for each activity, follow these steps:

1. Add the data.
2. Divide the sum by the total number of points, getting the average, just as when setting an intuitive goal. This average is called the "mean." The mean is a measure of central tendency. It shows how numbers tend to go toward the middle point.
3. Subtract each data point from the mean.
4. Square each answer. For example, if the mean is 12 and your data point is 8, subtracting 8 from 12 gives you 4. Square 4. The square is 16. Do this for each data point.

5. Add the squared amounts.
6. Divide the sum by the total number of data points, thereby getting an average.
7. Find the square root of the answer.

The answer is the standard deviation from the mean, or sigma. The sigma shows how representative the mean is of all of the data points. A large standard deviation suggests the data points are far apart. A small standard deviation suggests a small measure of dispersion between data points.

Your average, the mean, is the satisfactory goal level. Your minimum goal level is 1.5 times the standard deviation above or below the average, respectively. The outstanding goal level is 2.5 times the standard deviation above or below the average.

As an example, let's use the data David gathered for his intuitive goal, as explained in the previous section. We'll use the same data for setting a statistical goal, although David only gathered data for one week and a statistical goal should have more than one week's data.

David established two goals, each based on his supervisor's expectations (success areas) for the project: quantity and defect-free parts. David arrived at his numerical values by following these steps:

- (Step One) The sum of parts over a five day period is 750.
- (Step Two) The average, or mean, is 150.
- (Step Three) Subtracting each data point from the mean, David gets:
  150—145 = 5
  150—150 = 0
  150—140 = 10
  150—160 = -10
  150—155 = -5
- (Step Four) Square each answer:
  5 squared = 25
  0 squared = 0
  10 squared = 100
  -10 squared = 100
  -5 squared = 25

- (Step Five) Add the squared amounts:
  250
- (Step Six) Divide the sum by the number of data points:
  250 ÷ 5 = 50
- (Step Seven) Find the square root of the answer:
  Square root of 50 = 7.07 (or 7)

Now that we have this statistical information, use it to calculate a statistical goal for **# of parts produced per day**:

minimum / maximum: 1.5 * standard deviation (7) = 10.5 (rounded off to 11).
150 (mean)—11 = 139

satisfactory: 16 (mean)

outstanding: 2.5 * standard deviation (7) = 17.5 (rounded off to 18).
150 (mean) + 18 = 168

Compare David's intuitive goal values for **# produced per day** to his statistical goal values. Do you think one is more accurate than the other? Do you think he will have a harder time reaching his outstanding goal using one method over the other, or that he stands a better chance falling below his minimum expectations using one method than he would using another?

It is customary for the two sets of values to be very similar, so you are free to choose whichever method is more comfortable for you. However, the statistical method is, of course, more accurate.

■ Keeping Track of Goals—Your Scorecard

When everyone has finished setting minimum, satisfactory, and outstanding goal levels, have each person develop a scorecard that explains how he identified his goals. Everyone should carry their scorecards with them to keep track of progress. Encourage your employees to think about their entries on the scorecard and refine them. Any time someone experiences change in any of his critical relationships, success areas, or goals, he should rethink his numbers. The more accurate the goals, the greater the chance of being successful.

Here is a sample scorecard.

Scorecard for _____
Date
Company name

Critical Relationship	Type	Success Area	Goal	Unit	M	S	O

The following is a sample scorecard you might make for yourself:

Critical Relationship is the name of your critical relation. Use the actual name. For example, if this goal relates to your employer and Dixie Manufacturing owns your company, enter Dixie as your critical relation.

Type is the type of relationship it is, such as employer, supervisor, or supplier. In this example, it is employer.

Success Area is your activity that your critical relation is concerned about.

Goal corresponds to the numerical measurement of your performance of that activity.

Unit is the unit of measurement you use to categorize your goals. For example, enter "project" if the goals are for a particular project. You can also enter hour, day, week, or month.

M/S/O are your minimum, satisfactory, and outstanding goal levels.

On the next page is an example of a scorecard as filled out by Ed Blakely, a machinist at Lakeside Manufacturing.

Scorecard for Ed Blakely

Date June 1996
Lakeside Manufacturing

Critical Relationship	Type	Success Area	Goal	Unit	M	S	O
Lakeside	employer	reduce scrap	# parts discarded	daily	3	2	0
Jim Burke	supervisor	increase output	# parts produced	daily	22	25	35
		on-time schedule	# hours ahead of schedule	weekly	0	4	12
Larry Podreska	internal customer						

▪ Tracking Success

After setting three-level goals, people must track their progress. They can do this on a sheet of graph paper. Some businesses assign a person in the company to keep track of everyone's goals. This person, the librarian, collects everyone's data for each goal. This information can be collected either daily or weekly.

When each individual's information for each goal is collected, the librarian enters employees' data onto a graph, one for each goal. The librarian can then give the graph to each person or team that participates in the goal-setting process.

If your company doesn't have a tracking system, each person can chart his own success. Stationery stores have several types of graph paper. Select one that is easy to use and read. A good graph should show at a glance a person's progress toward his outstanding goal. It's important for a person to have a visual record, if possible, of his past and current performance that shows how his position changes each time new data is entered.

Interpreting Graphs

A data point is one data-mark on a graph or chart. Data points represent data gathered over a set period of time, and indicate how an individual or team has performed in relation to the numerical goal.

Here's how to read the data on the chart:

- The status is *positive* if two or more data points have been equal to or better than the satisfactory goal level more than once.
- The status is *negative* if two or more data points have been equal to or worse than the minimum level more than once.
- The status is *neutral* if all data points fall between the minimum and satisfactory level.

Below is a chart containing one week of data points. Notice the three horizontal bars on the graph. The lowest represents the minimum level (set at 11). The center horizontal line represents the satisfactory level, and the topmost horizontal bar defines the outstanding level. The first week of data points entered on the chart show that the status is negative, because two data points have fallen below the minimum level. But even though the first two data points show a negative status, the owner of this chart can take heart! The overall trend is upwards.

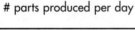

parts produced per day

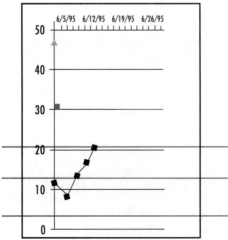

Using a Trend Line

When there are five points of data entered on the chart, set the trend line. A trend line shows the general direction in which the performance is moving.

Using a pencil and ruler, draw one straight line near the data points in the general direction they indicate, as shown in the diagram. Notice that the trend lines indicate a direction, either positive or negative. Progress is positive if the line slants toward the outstanding goal. Performance is decreasing (negative) if the line slants toward the minimum level.

If the trend line indicates a positive slant toward the outstanding goal level, mentally extend the trend line from where it is now to where it bisects the outstanding goal level. That intersection indicates the date by which a person should achieve his outstanding goal.

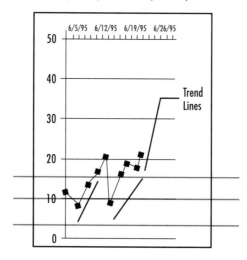

# of parts produced per day

Each time a person charts progress towards a goal by entering data on his chart, he should ask himself, "How did this happen?" Encourage your employees to reflect on how they achieved the results on their charts. They may want to repeat some of the behaviors that produced the results shown. Or they may need to take other steps that will change the direction of their performance. Whatever a person does, he should be moving toward his goal of outstanding performance.

Encourage people to follow up their chart review by asking open-ended questions that cannot be answered with a simple "yes" or "no." Such questions invite clarifications, explanation, and discussion. Conversation about how to achieve goals or improve performance is what you want to achieve. You may also want to show your employees your charts, and ask for their suggestions on what you can do to improve.

Giving effective feedback on data points goes a long way to moving your company toward success. When people know they are receiving objective information, guidance, and attention, they are more focused on achieving their goals. They move forward with confidence because they know what results they'll achieve by taking specific actions.

CASE STUDY   Eric Jefferson owned a job shop with 35 employees. Each month Eric reviewed shop and customer rejections, and posted the numbers on a chart. He called this his "Quality Chart" and displayed it in the break room.

Eric's Quality Chart illustrated the number of parts scrapped each month. One month the chart showed that 2,000 washers were scrapped. The next month the chart showed three transmission cases and four gear boxes scrapped.

It seemed to Eric the employees didn't pay too much attention to the chart and the scrap rates it illustrated. In fact, he overheard an employee saying, "This month looks better than last month. There are only seven parts scrapped this month."

That was not the point Eric wanted to make. Actually, 2000 washers scrapped was less of a write-off than the transmission cases. It was obvious to Eric that he had to change the chart to make it more indicative of the actual problem. The information on the Quality Chart was too erratic and not representational of the real issue.

Eric re-thought the chart. He concluded that quality shouldn't be measured in quantity, unless there was only one part involved. It had to be measured in the cost of the discrepant parts. The chart also needed a trend line—something to show the

(cont.)

machinists changes over time. Finally, the chart had to be more personal. Eric wanted those who viewed it to be able to take action on what the chart depicted.

To make his chart a more effective tool, Eric changed it to a "cost of scrap and rework" chart. He also added a new feature: the names of the top two machinists who had significantly reduced their scrap rate according to their goal of # of scrap parts.

Therefore, Eric's new chart listed the scrapped parts and the total dollar cost of the scrapped parts, and showed a dollar value trend line so employees could see, from month to month, whether the shop was actually decreasing its scrap rate. The chart also listed the two "winner-circle" machinists who had the lowest scrap rate.

Eric immediately noticed employee response. People liked seeing the dollar scrap amount because it conveyed an immediate, concrete message. Also, the chart conveyed the message that scrap-rate reduction was a priority in Eric's shop.

One day when Eric was in his office, one of his two supervisors asked him if she could implement a "cause of discrepancy" program, and initiate special training in set-up procedures and tooling design to reduce overall scrap rate. Eric was amazed at the request. He had attempted to initiate this type of program for years, but received no favorable response. Now his supervisor was asking for such a program!

Remember, an effective chart is one that conveys a meaningful message and inspires people to take action.

Chapter Summary

- Goals should be broken down into three numerical levels so that the goal setter can work progressively toward high-level results.
- In order to set realistic goals, collect data on current performance levels before setting intuitive or statistical goals.
- Use scorecards and visual charts to keep track of progress.

Chapter 9
Improving Performance

■ Importance of Good Performance

Now that your employees have identified their goals, it's up to you to motivate them to reach those goals. People perform well when they know where they're going and have a good idea of how to get there. They are motivated by the knowledge that their success will be recognized and appreciated along the way.

In most organizations a small percentage of people are excellent performers. A much larger percentage are average performers. Collectively, *average performance is not enough to move a business forward in a competitive environment.* Individually, average performance does not contribute to high self-esteem. People don't feel good about themselves when they are doing just enough to get by.

Management's number one goal is to turn people into top achievers so they reach their full potential on the job and achieve the kind of results that make a shop move ahead of its competitors. A manager's objective is star performance because star performance means profit.

■ Motivating People to Improve Performance

There are two basic schools of thought about motivation. According to one, people are what they are and don't really change much. We have to learn to accept people as they are. The second school of thought believes that our performance is derived from our thoughts, feelings, attitude, and values, and is a changing pattern that results from what happens to us in life. If we are encouraged, we do better. If we are criticized or belittled, our performance suffers.

Innovative managers subscribe to this second school of thought, that proper motivation and positive reinforcement lead to positive performance. You motivate a person with two objectives in mind:

1. To move the amateur to nonprofessional, the nonprofessional to professional, and the professional to expert.
2. To keep employees at the expert level.

Boosting performance is achieved, in part, by moving people as quickly as possible from amateur to expert level. Because increased performance translates to greater profit, no machine shop can afford people who consistently perform poorly or who remain untrained amateurs forever. Therefore, as manager, you must make certain you and your shop's foremen or supervisors effectively identify each person's performance level. Together, you must design a plan of action on how to move each employee up the scale from amateur to professional. If you leave some people at the amateur level, you do a great disservice to them and to your organization.

▪ From Amateur to Expert

People perform at four different levels, called *performance levels*. When you can identify each employee's level of performance, you can offer the type of guidance they need to become experts. A person requires a different type of guidance at each performance level. Giving the wrong guidance by misdiagnosing the performance level causes serious confusion.

Here are the four performance levels, and the type of guidance required by each:

Amateur	The amateur cannot know what he hasn't experienced. He may have enthusiasm, and you may see potential in him. Many of his actions are automatic, impulsive, or instinctive. He needs lots of training if he is going to be of value to the company.
	The amateur needs lots of guidance and attention. After some training, he settles in. He becomes part of the daily routine and begins to learn his job. Don't let him go off by himself. He expects you to keep an eye on him, and he needs clear instructions if he is to succeed.
Nonprofessional	The nonprofessional is occasionally inept, but he learns quickly because he wants to learn. He is becoming aware of his lack of knowledge, and may identify areas where he needs to improve.
	More training and experience quickly increase his know-how. He requires lots of attention from his supervisor, such as goal-setting assistance and positive reinforcement. He also becomes competent at certain activities and works well at selected tasks without guidance.
Professional	The professional can do certain things with great accomplishment and skill, but may not be able to see the whole picture. The professional machinist is capable and effective at machine set-up and operation, however, he may be missing some of the fine skills of machining.
	At this level, he needs his manager to be available for support and encouragement. He enjoys working by himself and seeing his job through from beginning to end, only occasionally needing guidance. When the pieces of what he's doing begin to come together, he becomes an expert. Be patient with professionals.

(cont.)

Expert	This is the level at which everyone should function. An expert works well with fellow workers and immediately understands how to lay out his work and get the job done. An expert machinist understands how to estimate, plan, program, set up, run, and finish a job. Experts become mentors, guides, and teachers. The expert does his job well enough to rarely need support from his supervisor. Of course, he still deserves your appreciation and acknowledgement.

It's critical for you to know where each of your employees are on their course from amateur to expert so you can provide appropriate guidance. For example, the expert requires very little supervision. If you interfere with the expert by telling him things he already knows, or giving guidance when none is needed, you belittle him. He may feel you don't trust him, or worse, that you don't respect his knowledge and ability. No expert works long under this condition.

On the other hand, the opposite occurs with the amateur and nonprofessional. If the amateur and nonprofessional are not given guidance, but are expected to produce at the rate and quality of an expert, they become frustrated and easily angered. They feel the company is unfair, and that they are being unreasonably pushed by an insensitive supervisor.

It's easy for the top person to fall into the trap of making too much of the expert's work. After all, the expert is producing perfectly, without much guidance. The expert and the top person can easily have in-depth discussions on the entire organizational process. They may become friends. If the manager praises the expert to the exclusion of the amateur, the amateur never becomes professional enough to develop because he usually loses interest in work and eventually quits. If the manager shows favoritism to the experts, he discourages the amateurs from assuming their valued place in the company.

In general, those who work for you must not see your attention as favoritism. They must see a sincere effort by you to train amateurs, guide nonprofessionals, review the work of professionals, and encourage experts.

▪ Qualities of an Expert

Experts share the following qualities:

1. They manage time well. Successful people divide their activities into high and low priorities. They refuse to take advantage of opportunities that don't fit their game plan. They are focused.
2. They enjoy working in groups. Star performers are eager to work with others, to assign and be assigned tasks, to discuss pros and cons with coworkers, and be inspired by the ideas and initiative of others. Ninety percent of business is working with others and they realize that their relationships with others is what builds success.
3. They delegate. Delegation is not dumping disagreeable tasks onto others, or abdicating responsibility. To delegate is to give the authority and responsibility of a task to someone who considers it worthwhile from their point of view. In this way the top performer demonstrates trust. He knows the person he assigned a task to will properly carry it out. He gives the person a chance to make a valuable contribution.
4. They demonstrate resilience. Top achievers are creative people who have the ability to bounce back. They are not afraid of failure. In fact, many creative experts prepare themselves for possible failure beforehand. Knowing that they can cope with the worst failure brings peace of mind and almost assures their success because they have carefully assessed possible poor outcomes and developed contingency plans. If they do fail, experts don't quit trying; they use their failures as lessons that help them succeed later.
5. They view business as art. Great performers discover their personal style and build on it. They consciously strive to master the art of business.
6. They are curious about and pay attention to everything. Nothing is dumb. They associate with "idea" people, recognizing that great ideas are often hidden in the silliest notions.

7. Top achievers don't allow time for worry. They don't have time to listen to the "inner voice" that criticizes and complains and tells them things can't be done. Worry gets in the way of concentration. Besides, one survey calculated that only eight percent of what a person worries about actually occurs. And when something negative does occur, it is rarely as bad as anticipated. Imagination embroiders gloom, so star performers don't allow themselves to think that way.

8. They are ordinary people doing great things. Star performers don't try to impress people.

9. They solve problems by attacking the problems, not the people around them. They avoid creating problems or tension among coworkers.

■ Signs of Readiness

Your people want to succeed. They want to break out of their comfort zone and become experts. Actually, they may be exhibiting signs of their desire to forge ahead. They may have already expressed one or more of the following opinions:

1. I am uneasy with my present situation. There must be more to this job than this. I need a change. I've got to stretch my wings.

2. I wish I could be more like my friend who quit his job and started his own business. I wish I could be in his position.

3. I have mastered this task. I'm tired of doing this. The money doesn't mean that much to me anymore.

4. I need to exercise my skills and talents. I have more to offer, and I know I can do more.

5. I really would like to help others reach their goals. I'd like to train people, show them what I know.

Look at each item. Idea number one expresses uneasiness with the present situation. Number two is a desire to be like someone else, to emulate a leader. Number three expresses boredom due to task mastery, number four is a desire to contribute more, and number five is a willingness to teach others.

When a machinist thinks one or more of the above thoughts, he is ready to become an expert. He is already poised for growth. Take action on these feelings. All he needs is to know that you're there to support and lead him. When you help turn a person into an expert, you help yourself, your company, and the employee.

▪ Developing Experts

Begin by sharpening your vision of your employees. Ask yourself the following questions, and take time to write down your answers. They will help you focus on what must be done to help your people do their best.

1. What motivates a person to become a star performer?
2. Why do some people work harder for one manager than for another?
3. Why do some machine shops get better performance from their people than other shops?
4. Why do some people start out as great performers but gradually become poor performers?
5. Do some basic behavior problems seem to be occurring in my company over and over again? If yes, why?
6. What is our turnover rate?
7. Are we losing valuable people we would like to keep?
8. What motivates each of my employees individually?
9. Who was responsible for hiring certain employees? What was the reason?
10. Do our people really have the skills they need to make our shop a success?

Your answers to these questions pinpoint motivational barriers common in most machine shops. When you begin offering solutions to the problems posed by your answers, your company will start turning around.

Outstanding performance doesn't just "happen." But a good manager can make it happen. With skill, you can move your employees from average to outstanding performance, from amateurs to experts.

■ The Right Motivators

Here's a list of some factors that help people become experts.

right tools	good attitude
compensation	pride
feedback	self discipline
reinforcement	self respect
training	drive
good work environment	respect for others
quality materials	trust
recognition	patience
right software	understanding

Review the list carefully and decide which factors in these two columns are under your control and which are directly under the control of the performer.

As you can see, the left-hand column represents external motivators that make people perform well. These are things you can easily provide for an employee. For example, if a machinist doesn't have the right tools, discuss his needs with him. If his request is reasonable, get the tools he wants.

If an employee needs training in a particular area or operation, consider sending him to school. Think about the skills, creativity, and imagination the person brings to your shop. If you don't want to spend money on training for fear that the person will quit and go to work elsewhere, consider the reasons the machinist would give for leaving your company. More money? Better working conditions? A more satisfying position? If he doesn't think he's paid enough and you value his potential, consider giving him a raise. Keep in mind that improving his skills and knowledge will be of benefit to your company, so give him the training and don't give him reasons to leave. Remember, you are in competition with other machine shops for the best of the skilled labor force.

The right-hand column contains internal motivators that make people perform well. You have no direct control over these characteristics, yet these values, thoughts, feelings, and attitudes are often far more important than the external factors. *These values make up character.* A good worker, therefore, nurtures these values in himself and reflects them toward others. Though you have no direct control over the development of these qualities—you cannot legislate or order them into existence—you are in the unique position of creating an environment in which your employees know how valuable these qualities are. When these attitudes are developed, everyone recognizes the difference, including your shop's customers.

■ Increasing Performance Through Leadership

Internal qualities are exclusively under the control of the individual. No one can control another's values or attitudes. But a good manager who is focused on results and has created the right motivating environment can help develop positive thoughts and feelings in those who work for him. This increases everyone's performance and hence their value to the company.

Increasing an employee's performance is done in two ways. First, if you take care of the external matters, such as tools, materials, good working environment, compensation, etc., the internal values gradually take care of themselves. As an example, if you reinforce performance by complimenting a person and sharing the good things he's done with others, it makes the person more self-assured and therefore builds self-confidence. If one of your machinists suggests a new way of doing something, acknowledge his creativity and vision. Self-confidence leads to better performance. If you train a machinist to use a new, state-of-the-art tool so he can perform his task better and faster, you will see improved results. He will feel pride in his work, and start aiming for even higher goals.

Second, when you, as company leader, develop positive internal qualities, values, and attitudes, you begin to instill those values in those who work for you. You become a role model for character. This change in your own work style is what's known as a "soft shift." A soft shift is a shift in management that is not mentioned or legislated. It is a change in attitude destined to affect the entire organization. And it must begin with the top person.

Changing the external is management. Changing the internal through example is leadership.

Don't underestimate the influence you have over others or minimize the effects of your positive qualities on those around you. When you strive to become a person of good character, possessing strong moral values, trustworthiness, kindness, patience, honesty, and friendliness, your subordinates will begin nurturing those same characteristics within themselves. This makes for a better company and a better working environment.

CASE STUDY   Wayne Borden owns an injection molding plant in a rural community outside of Dallas, Texas. He asked a consultant to come in and look over his operation, to work with him on focusing his employees on growth with the goal of implementing a team environment.

On the first visit to Wayne's shop, while walking through the plant with Wayne, an employee approached. The employee was very upset. He informed Wayne that the shop had made a mistake and ordered the wrong material for the job. Now the job was going to be behind schedule.

Wayne excused himself and went to investigate the incident. The consultant followed him to the employee's workstation. After reviewing the work order and material requirements, Wayne recognized that the operator had inadvertently picked up and used the wrong box of material. Wayne calmly instructed the employee as to what material to use. He pointed to the correct material, three pallets down from what the machinist had been trying to use.

Wayne made a note to himself to improve the material identification system used in the plant.

"What happened?" The consultant asked.

"The company coding on the box of material can be confusing at times." he said. "I'm going to work on improving that system. Maybe you'll have time to help me devise a new system."

The consultant asked Wayne what he does when his employees make mistakes and scrap parts.

Wayne answered, "I don't look so much at the mistakes they make, but at their attitude, aptitude, attentiveness, and attendance." He said. "These are what are important to me." And he added with a smile "After all, if you don't make mistakes, you're not doing anything."

Wayne had already established a "soft shift" in his shop which made the rest of the consultant's work relatively easy. In

(cont.)

fact, Wayne's easygoing, yet focused manner affected everyone. His door was always open. Employees were never afraid
of approaching him. He gave his shop foreman, Barry, considerable leeway in tooling and scheduling the jobs and getting
them out of the shop.

"It wasn't always like this," Wayne admitted. "When I was
younger, I was hotheaded. I pretended I knew everything. Sometimes I'd even threaten to fire someone on the spot. This wasn't
a nice place to work. But the boss at that time, who founded this
business and whom I eventually bought it from, took me aside.
He told me I was the main difficulty in the shop, not the machinists. He told me that if I would lead, they would follow. And you
don't lead by pushing, he said. You lead by acting the way you
want others to act.

"He also taught me that the employees were my greatest
asset—far more valuable than a work order or a finished
product.

"We have a good shop now. That's why I'm ready to move
forward."

In every company where the manager demonstrates good character, performance increases and so does profit. Competition becomes more sharply focused when energies formerly exhausted
in internal dissension become directed outward, toward the
marketplace.

When the opposite occurs—when corporate leadership is uncooperative, mean, petty, and dishonest—there are two outcomes.
First, everyone begins responding to and exemplifying these traits.
When this occurs the company can become a miserable place to
work. Gossip, backbiting, and pettiness flourish. The turnover
rate is high. No one is certain of his future with the company.
Most people avoid their supervisors, the very people with whom
they should be nurturing a relationship! Second, those valuable
employees who have integrity will leave.

Leadership

"Management is telling others what to do. Leadership is setting the example."

1. Avoid mediocrity. You were not born to be mediocre, so don't allow your life to be wasted through mediocrity. Do the best that you possibly can in everything you do.
2. Meet challenges. No matter how confused the scene or limited the resources under your control, meet challenges with enthusiasm. Great deeds have always been accomplished through overcoming obstacles. Pursue your goals and persevere until you succeed.
3. Focus on the positive. Daily life is filled with pleasant and unpleasant events and people. Focus attention on the positive aspect in all events and in everyone around you. More importantly, don't dwell on your problems or on the faults of others.
4. Treat others with dignity. Treat all people—black, white, yellow, brown, rich, poor, young, old, male or female—with the same courtesy, consideration, and respect. Be responsive to their cares and needs. Prejudice is a handicap.
5. Help others. Help people help themselves on their journey to success by encouraging them to set goals. After you do this, let them solve their own problems and learn through their own mistakes. Don't hinder them by interfering in the struggles they must face. This is how you can make a difference in their lives, and through them, in the future.
6. Listen. Listen actively to what people say, and acknowledge their opinions. This helps them feel good about themselves because they know how much you value and care for them.
7. Make your own decisions. Don't rely solely on the opinions of others. Never look at the world through other people's perspectives no matter who they are. Find your own information and draw your own conclusions. Never make judgments before finding the truth. There is no one in this world who is more qualified than you are to find the truth. And when you set your course, don't blame

(cont.)

Leadership . . . *(continued)*

others for anything that happens. Take charge of your own future.

8. Judge fairly. Don't keep silent when you see injustice. Speak out in support of justice without considering how it may affect your interests.

9. Practice brevity. We suffer from too much information, and too much talk. Learn to select the few facts you need to further your goals and develop your philosophy. Avoid irrelevant information. Speaking briefly and clearly means you are focused. Rambling wordiness, in speech and writing, usually demonstrates you haven't thought through what you are saying. Help your subordinates be brief in their explanations, too.

10. Consider the bad news as good news. Sometimes you need to hear bad news because if you don't know what's wrong you can't fix it. When you hear bad news, decide if you can change it into good news through your actions.

Work With Your Employees on Developing Values

Here's an effective exercise for developing your employees' leadership values. Meet with your top supervisors, or if your shop is small, hold a brief meeting with all your employees first thing in the morning. Explain the difference between management (changing the external) and leadership (changing the internal). Ask each person to write down one characteristic he would like to change in himself. No one has to show what he wrote, but by writing down an idea or thought, even if it is only one word, each person will have more of a commitment to the idea of making a change in himself.

Ask each person to come up with a plan on how to change that characteristic in himself so it will affect those around him. Tell everyone to come up with a list of specific actions he can perform that will demonstrate the internal change that is taking place.

Plan to meet again in one week. At that time, ask if anyone wishes to share the characteristic he wants to change, and the action plan he devised to make that change. Don't coerce people into divulging their answers, but if someone does wish to discuss what he has written and his plan, let him. Everyone will benefit by the discussion that follows. If no one wishes to speak, just talk about the overall purpose and importance of the exercise.

■ Helping a Person Develop a Personal Investment in the Job

Another way to motivate your employees is to encourage them to become involved in their future growth. An employee has a personal investment in his job when he is consulted about how the job is to be done, or when he is asked his opinion. He must be given some leeway to exercise his creativity in performance of the task.

A task must be important to the person who performs it. If it is important to the owner but not to the employee, it will never get done efficiently. You can help someone perceive a task as having meaning by showing how it's relevant to his entire job and emphasizing that the task is essential to his personal success.

To increase a person's dedication to a task so it will be done properly, you must: (1) recognize the good results of what he is doing, and (2) identify the ingenuity or initiative he used that made the task successful. Effective recognition by a higher-up lets an employee and his coworkers know that what he does is important and valuable to the company.

CASE STUDY Lynn works as an estimator in a large, departmentalized job shop. He spends most of his day in his office calculating the number of hours it will take to machine parts. When jobs fail to meet the estimated time, Lynn complains that the machinists on the floor are slow. He insists his estimates are accurate, and if the machinists would only work harder, the schedule could be met.

Scott is a machinist in the same shop. He spends most of his day trying to live up to Lynn's expectations. He complains that Lynn's estimates are too low, and that no one could meet these estimates. More importantly, Scott feels that Lynn is unwilling to cooperate and discuss changing his estimating methods.

The constant argument between Lynn and Scott over estimated hours has begun to affect the entire shop.

(cont.)

Recently, the shop hired a new manufacturing manager, Lou, who was determined to fix the problem. Lou called a shop meeting. He noted some of the problems he felt existed, and stated that he wanted to work toward solving them.

"I can't do this alone," Lou said.

When Lou suggested they discuss the subject of the discrepancy between Lynn's estimates and actual shop performance, he opened a can of worms. There was much debate with lots of finger-pointing and accusations. Lou quickly calmed everyone down and announced that the entire shop would begin solving the problem the following day.

Lou had handled this type of problem before. The main problem was that the machinists were not consulted when it came time to estimate the job, yet were expected to perform to the estimate. They weren't asked for advice when the job was planned by the planning department, yet were expected to "make it work."

Lou's first step was to devise an "input and accountability" system. If the machinists were going to be held accountable for the time required to machine parts, then they should have input into those requirements. His system allowed input from the shop floor for labor hours, planning, and tooling. To take the system full cycle, labor reports identifying the actual hours taken to do a job were routed back to the individuals who developed the plan.

Next, Lou met with Lynn. He explained to Lynn his plan of having the machinists involved in a project to estimate labor hours, planning, and tooling. He assured Lynn that Lynn was still the estimator, and that his estimate was final. Lou showed Lynn how he could learn from the machinists, since many of them had good ideas about how to do a job and how to save money. Lou asked Lynn to take all comments into consideration when he did the estimates.

Lou then talked to Scott and the other machinists. He explained that he wanted them to help look over Lynn's estimates, make recommendations, and route the estimate back to Lynn. All comments, Lou emphasized, would be taken seriously.

The next morning Lou called another meeting and explained his plan in detail. Everyone—even Lynn—agreed to give it a try, though Lynn was skeptical at first.

(cont.)

During the next few weeks, Lou reviewed the estimates. He was careful not to reprimand anyone when the results weren't good. Instead, he used the results as a tool to instruct and educate the workers. Every week he held a shop meeting where everyone reviewed the estimate and actual hours on all jobs—those that went well, and those that didn't. At these meetings Lou refused to accept finger-pointing or accusations. He only allowed discussion on problem solving.

After a few weeks of reviewing the results of each job, employees became quickly skilled at accurately estimating jobs, especially Lynn. When Lynn saw how much more accurate his estimates became, he willingly agreed to use the results of Lou's input and accountability system. He had developed a personal investment in doing his job right.

■ Communicating Trust

Nothing is more important than trust. Trust is an invisible superstructure in every organization. It's hard to put your finger on it when it is present, but, like quality, you immediately know when it's not there.

You can motivate your employees to the expert level by exhibiting trust. When a person knows you have his best interests at heart, that you recognize his potential and his present and future value to the company, and that you're willing to work with him, he moves confidently toward the expert level.

When an employee feels he is excluded in any way from the company's future, he begins to lose faith. Including a person in plans and schemes and inviting him to participate in discussions shows you trust him. You may even want an employee to listen in when higher-ups are making plans. A person is willing to share his creative ideas and put in extra hours when he knows his job is secure and he's a trusted part of the company's future. To an expert, job security is more valuable than a bonus or promotion.

One good way to ensure this trust is to speak privately one-on-one with each employee for 15 to 20 minutes (longer if possible) at least once a week. They will feel comfortable talking to you if you regularly visit with them. You make them feel important when you let them know their ideas are important. And most of all, listen to what they say!

Ask an employee to make a list of items he wishes to discuss with you before each meeting. Then listen carefully and quietly as your employee goes through his list of items. You may be surprised at some of the things employees choose to talk about, and their ideas will give you insights into your company's operations.

You, too, must develop a brief agenda covering items you wish to discuss with each of your employees, such as progress (or lack of progress) and company policies. You may also wish to share a bit of "inside information" about the company, the direction it's taking, and what you expect to accomplish and see in the future. Be sure to discuss each item, and ask for questions or comments.

The Danger of Asking "Why?"

Here's an important behavior you may wish to begin changing in yourself. It brings immediate results.

When asking a question, never use the word "why." Questions that begin with "why," such as "Why didn't you do this?," create defensive responses. In business, "why" is a threatening word. Instead of using "why," ask a "tell me" question, such as "Tell me the problems you had in getting this done."

As an example, which of the following questions would you rather hear—"Why are you behind schedule?" or "Tell me the reasons you're behind schedule on this item"?

Use this method to keep in touch. A one-on-one meeting, even a very brief meeting, is a strong tool toward helping a person achieve peak performance. A meeting such as this helps achieve trust because it is personal and focused toward the best interests of the employee, owner, and the company as a whole.

■ Pitfalls of Being a "Technical" Manager

It's usually very difficult for a technical person, one who has come up through the ranks and now runs his own shop, to keep from interfering in others' work. It's even harder for such a person to learn to manage people, not products or services. The manager with a technical background must learn to motivate people—inspiring them, helping them solve their problems, being present when needed, and gaining trust—without taking over their work. Mismanaging your employees will drive them away.

Quite often the technical manager finds himself interfering with the work process. The reason, of course, is that he developed expertise when he was on the front line. When he sees less-than-expert performance, his inclination is to roll up his sleeves, reach over the shoulder of a nearby machinist, and help him do it the "right" way.

This is the most common reason many large corporations hire managers from outside the company rather than promote from inside. Someone from the outside is often less inclined to interfere with established processes. He focuses more on results rather than the processes people go through to get those results. You must learn to change the process only when results are not forthcoming.

The key to your success in business is to learn to motivate your employees without dominating them. In striving for the results you want, focus on managing the outcome, not the process. The process is how the job is done, not what is finally accomplished. When you attempt to manage the process—when you interfere with the way things are done—you create immediate disenchantment and suspicion. You should trust a subordinate to be professional enough to have his own appropriate, reliable method of getting the job done.

When you attempt to manage the way someone does his work, he may feel you are meddlesome and condescending. He might lose self-respect and become upset. His negative attitude then affects his coworkers. Instead of seeking you out for needed advice, he avoids contact with you, assuming you won't work with him on achieving results. When this occurs his work may noticeably suffer. He may even sabotage his own efforts.

Even with amateurs and nonprofessionals, who expect and require guidance and training, you and the shop's supervisors must take care to focus on results. Monitor the work of amateurs and nonprofessionals, but let them work out the details of their processes. The professional and the expert can manage their own work because they know what's expected of them.

Help employees focus on results, but let them solve their own problems and establish their own methods. Keep an observing eye on their work, but interfere only when their results get off track. Everyone will appreciate your unobtrusive involvement—lending a hand, giving advice, and voicing encouragement.

■ Why Some People Fear Success

Although you may be striving to effectively motivate your employees, you may encounter some resistance. One barrier to becoming an expert is the fear of success.

The fear of success can be so powerful that a person is willing to live in a comfort zone where he doesn't have to challenge himself. When a person is mired in this comfort zone for some time, he eventually develops a sense of uneasiness about his job, a feeling of a lack of personal fulfillment, a growing boredom. Few attempt the creative risks necessary to challenge themselves to break free of this comfort zone. Quite often it takes the attention of another person, such as the shop's owner, manager, or supervisor, to help an employee recognize his own potential for success.

There are several characteristics common to those who fear success:

1. Avoidance of making decisions that involve risk-taking. No matter how safe the risk, it's easy to find an excuse to avoid decision making.

2. Fear of disappointing others' high expectations. When a person operates at a low level there are few people to disappoint. When a person becomes successful it's easier to let employers and powerful acquaintances down. After all, they begin to expect top work, good ideas, and timely solutions to problems. If a person doesn't always produce at the level others expect, he may feel they will begin to question his ability.

3. Fear that increased success will alienate friends and peers. For example, someone may wonder what his friends will think if he begins to excel. By moving "up the ladder," he will be making new friends, moving in different circles. Going from a machine operator to a foreman can bring on some unwelcome comments and changes.

4. The ever-present and common fear of the unknown. Everyone has this fear. If someone works all his life in a comfort zone, he builds a protective wall around himself. He always knows what to expect. His activities are predetermined. To reach for new horizons, he must break free of his own limitations—plunge into the unknown—in order to dissolve the comfort zone.

5. Most importantly, there is the fear of getting to know oneself. It's difficult for some people to confront their own personal development. It's easier to avoid self-knowledge and stay on the known path. When someone begins to test himself, to measure his potential, this challenging and frightening idea occurs: "If it is really true that I have this capacity, then what else don't I know about myself?"

▪ Helping Employees Overcome the Fear of Success

As manager or shop owner, you want to move employees as quickly as possible from the amateur to the expert level. You cannot do this if the employee is reluctant to move because of a fear of success. To help a person overcome this fear and gain the confidence needed to become an expert, consider the following:

- Give some decision-making responsibilities. Encourage a reluctant employee to make certain decisions about his tasks.
- Don't be disappointed with the employee's decisions once you've given him the responsibility of making them. Give encouragement. If an employee's decision produces unfavorable results, explain why. This is how he learns.
- Encourage cooperation among employees, not competition. Cooperation produces a greater degree of security. In a cooperative environment people feel less threatened by their peers; more accepted for being who they are. On the other hand, competition typically creates a negative environment of winners and losers. And the losers are not necessarily the least accomplished employees. You want all of your employees to feel like winners.
- Recognize accomplishment. A word of praise, an announcement on the breakroom bulletin-board, or a reward goes a long way to encourage an employee.

- Put people in positions where they can experience success. Give them tasks they can accomplish, then move them up to more challenging tasks.
- Focus on success. Use the word "success" frequently. It's a word that you can't over-use. No one gets tired of hearing it.

CASE STUDY

1974 . . .

Deerfield Manufacturing, near Detroit, was tied into the automobile industry. Deerfield hired Tyrone Holloway right out of college, where he graduated with an engineering degree. They had high hopes for him. He got good grades in school, and had a good background in shop operation, having worked summers since high school in various shops in Detroit. He was outgoing and personable.

Tyrone was content to start out as a machinist, with the agreement that he would be given first consideration for a supervisory position.

After six months, the quality of Tyrone's production was good, but his output was low. His supervisor, Bob, a veteran in shop management, tried various techniques to help Tyrone increase his output. He scheduled Tyrone's week so that he would have time to put things in order and arrange his work-site. He helped Tyrone manage his stock on hand. He worked with Tyrone to review equipment and tools.

Bob eventually turned in an evaluation report to the manager and co-owner, Neil. It did not have good things to say about Tyrone. The report mentioned that Tyrone was a careful worker, but was slow. He knew the theories behind what he was doing, but didn't seem to organize his work very well. Bob also reported that Tyrone talked a lot with fellow workers—maybe too much. He was well-liked in the shop and was friendly with everyone, but seemed to only have half-interest in his work.

Neil called Tyrone into his office to discuss the evaluation.

It didn't go too well. Tyrone was disappointed by Bob's evaluation of his work, but didn't deny that he was a poor producer, or that Bob hadn't worked hard with him.

Neil asked what Tyrone thought should be done about the situation—how they could remedy it. "I want you to be successful," Neil said.

(cont.)

Tyrone seemed uncomfortable. "Maybe I'm not cut out for this kind of work."

"You have a degree in engineering!" Neil said. "You wouldn't have pursued that degree if you didn't have aptitude and interest for this kind of work!"

Tyrone sighed. He had no answers.

Neil came up with the answer.

1996 . . .

In a recent discussion with Neil, now owner of Deerfield Manufacturing, he said, "I owe a lot of Deerfield's success to Tyrone. I almost fired him at one point—he just couldn't succeed as a machinist. It's almost as if he wanted to fail. We tried everything. It seemed as though he was sabotaging his possibility for success.

"But I didn't want to let him go. I knew he had potential. There was something about him, his personality, his thoughtfulness. Whatever it was, I had an idea about how to capitalize on it and it was the best idea I ever had.

"We had a senior salesman at the time whose name was Dick something. I told him to take Tyrone with him, have him meet our customers, see if he could catch on to sales. After all, he knew our product well enough after four years of college. I thought maybe he'd be better at sales, and I wanted to give him one more chance to succeed.

"Anyway, Tyrone has turned out to be our number-one salesman. We wouldn't be where we are today without him. And you know what he sells? He doesn't sell our product. He sells concern. He sells care. He sells personal attention.

"He calls it 'soft' selling, as opposed to 'hard' sales, which is product sales. By selling concern, you can sell anything. I tell you, there have been instances where we've come in as the high bidder on a job, but the customer chooses us because they know Tyrone is here, and he has sold them on the concern we have. We have concern for the product we sell, and we have concern for the customer we sell it to. And Tyrone started this. He was lousy on the shop floor, but the moment we turned him loose in the field, he became a giant. Lots of our customers don't say 'Call Deerfield for an estimate.' They say, 'Call Tyrone, see what he says.'"

Chapter Summary

- You must learn to motivate your employees in order for them to get the results that will keep your shop competitive.
- Learn to identify what performance level your employees are working at—amateur, nonprofessional, professional, expert—so that you will know how much guidance and support they need and expect from you.
- Learn to recognize the qualities and signs that an employee is ready to become an expert; encourage and motivate that employee to do so.
- Provide all the external motivators you can, and create a work environment in which employees strive to develop their own internal motivators—character, leadership skills, and a personal investment in work.
- Always convey your trust in your employees' abilities.
- Help your employees break out of their comfort zones and overcome their fear of success.

Chapter 10
Reinforcement and Rewards

▪ Encouraging the Right Behavior

To motivate your employees to give you the behavior you admire, give immediate feedback—the good news and bad news about performance. A person needs to know how he's doing so he can be sure he's on the right track or make the necessary adjustments.

For example, if a machinist sets up an operation and runs the parts in an acceptable amount of time, recognize his performance. Praise his good work. If he falls short of expectations, discuss this with him. Make sure he gets the tools, training, and motivation he needs so he can become an expert.

Excellent managers provide frequent and high-quality feedback. For this feedback to be useful to someone, it must have these three general qualities:

- ▪ Addresses goals
- ▪ Reinforces behavior
- ▪ Provides direction

▪ Three Types of Reinforcement

There are three types of reinforcement you can give to generate positive results:

Positive Reinforcement	Positive reinforcement either initiates behavior you want or increases existing desired behavior. When a person has the training and tools he needs to do his job, and you've explained what you want done and when you want it done, reinforce his actions. Positive reinforcement lets him know he's doing it right.
Negative Reinforcement	Negative reinforcement discourages behavior you don't want. It lets a person know where he's going wrong, and shows him how his behavior is negatively affecting his performance and his coworkers. Negative reinforcement can be a warning that he better start doing it right if he wants to succeed.
Neutral Reinforcement	No reinforcement is neutral reinforcement. You may disapprove of some behaviors but don't want to make an issue of them; you would rather just watch them fade away and die. If this is the case, just ignore the behavior. Use neutral reinforcement when you want behavior to stop gradually. If it doesn't fade away, use negative reinforcement to discourage it, or positive reinforcement to initiate other behavior.

Review the accompanying illustration. Positive reinforcement increases behavior by supporting and encouraging that behavior. Negative reinforcement stops behavior, through criticism or a flat-out warning statement. However, neutral reinforcement (no reinforcement at all), represented by a wavy line, stops behavior

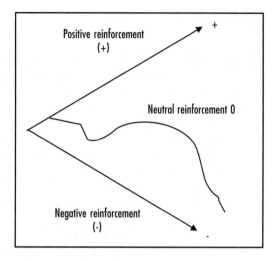

over time. Notice the line may sometimes rise, and sometimes dip, but the overall trend is downward.

The Importance of Positive Feedback

"Positive" feedback contains good information about a behavior or action a person has done that is really great—so great that the shop owner, or someone else whose opinion matters, stops by to comment on it. When a person receives good information, he can use it to achieve the same or better results next time. Positive feedback ensures continued top performance.

When a person receives good information about how he did, he will frequently share the feedback with others so they can get praise, too. This feedback usually starts a good chain reaction throughout the company.

Failure to reinforce good behavior is a dangerous thing, and it happens more frequently than you'd imagine. If you don't reinforce good behavior, your employee will see it as punishment. You run the risk of eventually extinguishing behavior you may want.

CASE STUDY   Jerry Hart, a machinist at a shop that manufactures aircraft parts, was asked by his supervisor to work overtime to finish parts that were critical for one of the company's most important customers. Jerry worked all weekend on the parts and finished them on Sunday afternoon. He was very proud that his supervisor trusted him with this important assignment.

First thing Monday he put the parts on his supervisor's desk. He waited for some type of recognition from his supervisor. Nothing. Tuesday came and went, and still the supervisor did not acknowledge his weekend efforts.

At first Jerry made excuses for his supervisor. He thought the supervisor might be too busy to get to him. Maybe something else came up and the supervisor had to attend to it.

Eventually Jerry became disheartened. He felt he had been taken advantage of. In fact, he started to avoid his supervisor, the very person he should be nurturing a relationship with!

What will happen the next time the supervisor asks Jerry to do some critical job? Will he be eager to do it? Will he work as hard on it? Will he give up his weekend to produce it? Positive, productive behavior that gets no response or recognition will gradually diminish.

The most common error shop owners make in managing people is failing to give positive reinforcement (encouragement), which is—by default—giving no reinforcement at all. Ignoring a person's good work because "that's what I pay him to do" diminishes his output and quality workmanship over time. Conversely, inadvertently rewarding a worker for non-performance by failing to give negative feedback will encourage him to engage in the undesirable behavior.

It's also important for you to be close enough to your employees so that you give recognition to the proper people. Don't allow one worker to take credit for another's work.

Understanding Negative Reinforcement

Bad behavior, such as routinely poor judgment, sloppy work, careless attitude, and lack of attention to details, is more infectious than good behavior. Unfortunately, when poor workmanship takes root it can spread quickly throughout an organization—far more quickly than good behavior. When an employee sees a coworker who has a poor attitude and bad work habits receive the same pay and attention he receives, he thinks, "Why should I work so hard? I'm making the same money he's making. Besides, the supervisor doesn't seem to notice. He lets him get away with it." The result may be that the diligent worker begins to let his own work slide as well.

Feedback that comments on what a person is doing wrong and how to change it for the better should be looked upon as good news. This feedback, often called "negative" feedback, is really information that helps a person do better next time. Negative feedback is essential for identifying counterproductive or dangerous behavior and stopping it as quickly as possible.

An expert cherishes negative feedback. It helps him fine-tune his skills. When negative feedback is directed toward achieving goals, a smart person can use the information to adjust his behavior in order to reach his goals. It may even cause him to rethink his critical relationships, success areas, or goals.

Using Neutral Reinforcement

Occasionally, you may disapprove of a person's behavior, but before you say anything, you must decide if it really affects coworkers and his own results in a negative way. If it doesn't, try and ignore it. It may not be important, and may even gradually disappear because it hasn't been reinforced. If it is detrimental, take action!

Smart managers guide people toward success by reinforcing good behavior, acknowledging all efforts, stopping bad behavior, and knowing when to let harmless things slide by. They don't overreact to insignificant idiosyncrasies.

▪ Getting Started with Reinforcement

Behavior, both good and bad, is triggered by a cue or prompt. For instance, the arrival of a supervisor in the work area may be a prompt for people to start working harder. A memo in the office mailbox can be a prompt for turning in an expense report. The appearance of a police car when driving home is a cue to check your speed—maybe even to slow down!

An inexperienced manager frequently makes the mistake of managing by prompts. In other words, he tries to elicit certain behaviors, meanwhile losing sight of the need to get certain results. A prompt only gets the behavior going; feedback keeps the behavior going and leads to results. An experienced manager wants to see results, and makes certain the whole shop is organized to get those results. Decide what cues or prompts you can use to get the behavior going, but be sure to follow up with reinforcement to achieve the desired results.

Some cues you can give to get the right behavior going may be simple statements, such as:

- "I'll come by at 11:00 a.m. to see how you're doing."
- "When you've finished with this project, stop by my office."
- "If we can get this project done by October 16th, then we'll get the follow-on order from the customer."
- "Now that you've gotten this far, here's what to do next."

In each of these examples, you are merely starting behavior to get results. Once you've used these prompts, move on to reinforcement.

▪ When and Where to Give Feedback

It's not necessary to have a pre-scheduled appointment when giving positive feedback. Spontaneity is important. In fact, spontaneity is desirable. Irregular but frequent visits to a department or to a machinist, operator, or any employee is much more effective and appreciated than scheduled events. People are often more eager to talk about things when you casually drop by their workstations. It's also more relaxing than meeting around a table at a special time.

However, negative feedback should be given on neutral turf— not your office and not the employee's workstation either. A neutral location, such as a lunchroom or empty conference room, is usually less threatening. You will stand a better chance of getting your point across, and the employee will have a better chance of understanding your point without being distracted.

■ The Basics of Giving Feedback

Begin by following these three simple steps to use reinforcement:

1. Identify the behavior you want to change or encourage.
2. Reinforce that behavior using negative, positive, or neutral reinforcement.
3. Expect results.

Feedback must be proportional to the subject at hand. You don't want to sound insincere, flattering, or overly complimentary. Also, make sure the feedback you give is information a person can use to increase his value to the company. This is very important. Don't give feedback because you're a nice guy or you want to be everyone's chum. You must give specific information on an accomplishment. For instance, don't say, "You're doing a good job." It's always nice for a person to hear that, but it really doesn't mean anything. Instead, say, "I see you've almost reached your goal. And your work has been free of discrepancies. This is really turning things around."

When you give feedback, keep it focused. The more specific, the better! Feedback is most effective when related to specific behavior. As another example, it's better to say, "We've been able to ship the order two days early, thanks to your efforts. This is a great service to our customer," rather than saying, "Production sure has improved."

The more data you have to support your feedback, the more meaning it has for the employee. Words like "excellent" or "superior" are subject to interpretation. For example, when a person is shown statistics that he's achieved a 5% improvement over previous best performance, the meaning is clear. Actual data proves your point.

A number that reflects the performance of a thousand people has far less impact than a number that reflects the performance of a team of three. It doesn't hurt to display a chart or poster that reflects the company's overall production. But it's more effective to show the accomplishments of an individual or team.

Feedback must be related to the employee's goals, otherwise it is too subjective and has little meaning. There's nothing wrong with subjective feedback; it's just that none of us see the whole picture. We are all influenced by personalities, immediate events, and how we are feeling that day. As an example, a shop owner might think a machinist is the greatest machinist in the world, and the shop owner is grateful to have hired him. The owner might lavish praise on this individual and hold him up to others as an ideal, only to find out later he's not as good as everyone thought. That's because there was no objective way to measure his activities.

Reinforcement must be immediate, that is, it must come on the heels of the behavior. Don't necessarily wait until Friday or pay-day to give praise.

Good reinforcement must also be personal, not general. Use the name of the person whose behavior you're reinforcing. Look him in the eye. Make certain he knows the reinforcement is meant for him.

However, always be sensitive to the individual when giving reinforcement. Praise and criticism must fit the person's character. If a person is embarrassed by special attention, give positive rein-forcement privately. This is very important because a person can be embarrassed or hurt when reinforced at the wrong time. Here's an example: Let's say a machinist has been making good progress in learning to operate a new CNC machining center. If you give this machinist praise in front of his peers, he may become embar-rassed, even though your intention was to show your pleasure in his progress. Words you meant as praise might have the opposite effect. Therefore, with this employee, it would be better to give positive reinforcement privately.

While most feedback is verbal, you can give effective positive feedback in other ways, too. For example, consider writing a memo and posting it on a bulletin board. If you're a manager, write a statement about someone's successful achievement to-ward his goal and send it to the employee, or have it included in the company newsletter.

Another way to give effective feedback, especially when giving feedback to a team, is to display a graph or chart. Show the specific numbers that reflect their accomplishment. A visual dis-play means something to everyone. It's a constant reminder of success.

■ How to Give Negative Feedback

If an employee needs discipline because of improper or disruptive behavior, explain in specific terms what he has done that you disapprove of and what behavior or performance you expect. Believe it or not, the employee may not know a problem exists, and therefore, doesn't realize his actions are inappropriate. After all, he has a very subjective view of what's going on. You have to tell him that a problem exists, what the problem is, and why it is a problem. Keep your comments short, not more than a few sentences. Don't drag out an explanation which may induce argument, denial, or anger.

Here's an example of stopping unproductive behavior. Let's say one of your machinists is habitually late for work. You want him to arrive at work on time. Ask yourself what happens when he comes in late. What are the results of his behavior? Does he get yelled at by a supervisor? Do coworkers joke with him about his being late and therefore encourage his bad behavior?

Don't consider why the employee is late, regardless of his excuse. Consider only the results of his lateness. Five minutes late a day means putting production behind. He may be holding up an assembly line, or forcing others to wait on his behalf, thereby tying up a whole department. His tardiness can put the whole plant behind schedule. A person who is habitually late for work demoralizes those on-time workers around him.

In general, habitual lateness demonstrates unwillingness to participate. When we really don't want to be somewhere, we drag our feet and show up late. When we really want to be somewhere, we're usually early. People who are early or on time indicate eagerness to participate.

Explain what the results of this continued behavior will be. Use an "If..., then..." statement to achieve this. Any directive *not* using "If..., then..." has little effect on changing behavior. Say, "If you have trouble getting up in the morning, then buy a decent alarm clock. I expect you here at 8:00 a.m." Or, "If you are late one more time, then I'm moving you to another department. You will lose accumulated sick pay." Or you may be forced to say, "If you can't get to work on time, then I must find someone else to do your job." This stimulates the behavior you want.

After reprimanding, don't hold a grudge, and never mention the incident to the employee again, unless the behavior does not stop. And never mention the employee's unsatisfactory behavior to anyone else. It's no one else's business. The incident is between you and your employee. Make this assumption: I have reprimanded this employee. I pointed out what I don't want, and why I don't want it. He won't do this again.

When giving negative feedback, give the individual a chance to make changes. This shows respect. Suggest several changes he may wish to consider. Negative feedback is successful when the person receiving it can decide how to change his own activity and then see the results of his new behavior.

Never degrade a person by calling him names, or inferring he is lazy or incompetent. This will never make him want to do better. It will only make him resentful. Focus on the *problem* from the standpoint of productivity and company morale, not the *person*.

Try to phrase negative feedback in positive terms. Amateurs and nonprofessionals often view negative feedback as personal criticism because they have not learned to interpret feedback as knowledge they can use. Emphasize that now that the employee knows what's wrong, he can fix it.

CASE STUDY   Tim was in a setup on a vertical machining center when the foreman stopped by and asked Tim's opinion on how he'd run a new job that was being bid. Tim, an experienced machinist, reviewed the job with the foreman and offered his opinions. When Tim returned to his setup he inadvertently pushed the wrong button. The cutter sliced into the part Tim was setting up, turning it to scrap.

When the foreman reviewed the situation and wrote out a rejection tag, he labeled the cause of the scrap as "operator error." When he presented the tag to Tim, Tim calmly explained that if he hadn't been interrupted and lost his concentration, he probably wouldn't have made the mistake. He told the foreman that distractions, particularly during setups, were hard for him to deal with. He told the foreman he was glad to offer his opinion on how to run a job, and would help any way

(cont.)

he could. However, he asked the foreman to wait until he was finished with a setup before he asked his advice.

The foreman agreed with Tim. He used this "negative" information to set a personal goal to avoid interrupting the machinists when they were doing setups unless absolutely necessary.

A further benefit came from this encounter. In discussion with the foreman on this issue, Tim pointed out that the term "operator error" is misleading. When scrap is tagged with a rejection slip, the cause of discrepancy should be far more detailed. To say "operator error" implies anything, from operator carelessness to operator incompetence.

"How would you tag this piece?" The foreman asked.

"Just say something like, 'Operator was interrupted during setup. When he returned to job he inadvertently pressed the start button before the setup was completed.'"

The foreman saw how this detailed information on the rejection tag would benefit everyone in the shop when they discussed discrepant parts.

In this instance, an experienced employee used criticism—negative feedback—to improve the way he interracted with coworkers and to improve a scrap identification procedure. The negative information was used to make positive changes.

Finally, negative reinforcement should always be given privately, away from others' ears.

▪ Reinforcement Pitfalls

When you identify a behavior or result you like and give positive reinforcement, never conclude by saying "and give me more." When you ask for more of the same behavior, you're telling the person that what he's doing is more important to you than who he is as a person. This is demeaning. It detracts from his motivation to do a good job. A person needs to know that he is associated with the job he's doing and that both he and the task are important.

Also, never give positive reinforcement and negative reinforcement at the same time. Keep them separate. Giving both at the same time cancels the benefit of each and gives mixed messages. For instance, think about how you'd feel if your supervisor said to you, "Thanks for staying late and finishing this job. I know the customer will really appreciate it, and I intend to tell him you worked late to meet his deadline. But clean up around here! Your area is always a mess!" Obviously, the encouraging word is badly overshadowed by the personal criticism. If you feel you must comment about the clutter in the workplace, give this guidance at a time and place removed from the praise.

Some may interpret your attention to a certain person who performs well as favoritism. To avoid this, explain to everyone, especially the person you're giving reinforcement to, that the behavior is important to you and is required for success in your shop.

Three Types of Problems

If you assign a task and the employee doesn't perform at the expected level, you must determine what kind of problem you're dealing with. It will be one of three types:

- The "can't do" problem, in which the employee honestly can't perform the assigned task. You must determine what training, time, tools, and equipment he needs to perform the task adequately.
- The "won't do" problem, in which the employee refuses to do as you ask, even if you plead or threaten. "Won't do" problems usually arise when the employee's past good performance was not reinforced, when he doesn't see the importance of performing the task, or when you have not set the proper example for him.
- The "can't be done" problem, which usually turns out to be an impossible task that shouldn't have been assigned in the first place.

When you encounter resistance of any kind, your first step should be to discuss the problem with the employee. Listen intently to what he is saying. Then, categorize and solve the problem accordingly, especially if it requires a change in your behavior.

■ Learning to Accept Feedback

Even though you're the top person in the shop, you should be comfortable receiving feedback from subordinates. Stimulate the flow of information in both directions. Don't fear their criticism; welcome it! It's just as appropriate for an employee to give an owner or supervisor feedback as it is for the owner or supervisor to give a machinist feedback.

Of course, you must set up the right environment for this exchange to take place. You may want to consider a group meeting once a week at a designated time to discuss goals and how everyone's doing. If possible, hold the meeting in a neutral place where everyone is comfortable. At the end of the meeting, after reviewing everyone's goals, ask your people how they think you are doing. You might want to show them your goal progress chart and discuss your goals with them. After all, your progress reflects on how well they are doing!

When discussing your goals with machinists and others in your shop, remember that the front-line workers are often best able to judge how a specific job is going. They are the closest to all of the unique details of a job and the shop. They are often the first to know when things are headed in the wrong direction, and they frequently have ideas on how to turn things around. Your overriding goal (corporate goal) is to increase production, and to do this you must listen to your employees, support your people, solve problems, and keep everyone going in the same direction.

CASE STUDY   Wayne Semona is the manufacturing engineer in a large Boston job shop. His duties are to oversee the planning, CNC programming, and tooling departments. Wayne has been doing this job for some time. People expect a lot from him, and Wayne runs from department to department, working hard to coordinate efforts.

Over time, Wayne began ridiculing the shop's quality department. As far as he was concerned, they could do no good. Any mistakes they made, Wayne was sure to augment and spread throughout the shop. When the manager of the quality department confronted Wayne about the complaints, Wayne wouldn't listen. He just made more disparaging comments.

Wayne's complaints about the quality department began to put everyone in a bad mood. Other workers began to complain.

(cont.)

Bill MacIntyre was an old timer. He had been cranking handles and pushing buttons for over 20 years. At first Bill didn't say anything when he heard the complaints. He continued to do his work.

One day Wayne stopped by Bill's workstation and gruffly stated that they would be way ahead of schedule if it weren't for the incompetence of the quality department, which was always ready to jump on any insignificant detail.

Bill said, "Wayne, I've been here for years, and I've learned a few things. One is this. Criticism is infectious. It might start with one person or one department, but pretty soon it spreads like a disease throughout the shop. Then everyone is being critical and trying to make the other guy look like the incompetent one. No one wants to work in surroundings like that.

"Now I know you've had some disagreements with the quality control department, and surely they make mistakes. But they're trying to do their job, too. I see morale slipping away quickly here in production. If you don't do something to turn it around, you're going to have big problems. People will start to leave. No one wants to work in a place where blame predominates. It's harder to solve problems than to blame others for the problem, but it's what you've got to do."

Wayne had worked with Bill for years and respected his insights. He and Bill spoke further about the situation brewing in the shop.

"You're right," Wayne admitted. "I'm going over to quality control right now to see how we can work out a few of these problems."

▪ Rewarding Results

Once you start seeing the results you hoped to inspire, reward your employees for those results. Actually, the amateur and non-professional must be recognized more for the behavior or steps they are taking to achieve results. They must be recognized for trying, for making the effort. But the professional and expert should be rewarded for their results. Encourage the behavior through reinforcement, but give rewards for the results.

However, keep in mind that even an expert occasionally must be rewarded for the small things he does, for behavior he doesn't even think about. For instance, an expert may show up a half-hour early each day to lay out his work. He considers being early part of his job. If being early is a behavior you admire because it contributes to his results, reward him for this behavior or at least recognize it.

Compensation is what you give people for what they do. Rewards are what you give people when they do well.

■ Two Types of Rewards

There are two types of rewards: tangible and nontangible. You can use both types of rewards to celebrate results. It's important to know the power behind each type of reward, and when to use the right type.

Tangible rewards are concrete and observable. Nontangible rewards are less material and less precise, but in most cases, far more effective.

Tangible Rewards

Tangible rewards are specific things people work for, and they cost money. To receive a tangible reward is a confirmation to the person who receives the reward that in the eyes of his employer, he's achieving the right results. He's moving in the right direction, toward the expert level. A tangible reward is a valuable tool because it puts employees on notice. It lets them know that a specific, consistent behavior is appreciated and doesn't go unrecognized by the shop's management.

Of course, you decide whether a reward should be given, and when, as well as what type of reward should be given. It's up to you. One guideline for giving a tangible reward is to make certain you are rewarding a specific result, and that the person you are rewarding knows it is for a certain act he has performed.

When giving tangible rewards, don't be general or make the reward commonplace. For instance, don't tell everyone that coming to work early will result in a specific reward. Give a reward privately to someone who has earned special recognition. Rewards are usually most effective when given privately.

Some tangible rewards are:

> Raise
> Time off with pay
> Bonus
> Extra vacation days
> Profit sharing

Nontangible Rewards

Nontangible rewards are rewards that don't cost money, or at least not very much. Nontangible rewards are more effective and much more valued by employees than tangible rewards.

It's a mistake to think that money is the only type of reward that people want. Money is not the best reward because:

1. There's never enough of it. No matter how much you give, it's not enough. Everyone always needs more money.
2. It's not tied into immediate performance. When an employee does a specific behavior you like, and you give him money, he views that as a bonus for the entire job, not for a specific task. For reinforcement to be effective, it must be immediate and specific, clearly tied to a task.
3. It can become the only motivator. When money becomes the only motivator, quality suffers. People have no desire to work together; they are in competition for dollars.

CASE STUDY   William Franks, a foreman at Westchester Milling, suggested to his boss that the company go to a "merit" system to encourage actions he felt would produce results. A merit was a permanent pay raise, not a bonus. Bill's boss told him to devise a set of standards by which he could grade his machinists and then initiate the merit system.

At first the merit system was very popular. But it was Bill himself who began to see the danger inherent in his own system. He sent this memo to his boss: "Advise discontinuing merit system. People are doing what they have to do to get a pay increase, then slacking off. Therefore, overall production is declining."

4. It can be regarded as demeaning. Most people don't work just for money. They work to be recognized because they've done a good job. They have a need to be appreciated. They work to become an expert.
5. One must usually do something wonderful to get money. Many actions you want to reinforce are not "wonderful" in the big sense. They are small steps to getting the results you want.

Nontangible rewards are treasures. Everyone needs them! Here's a list of some effective nontangible rewards you can use to reinforce behavior.

Pat on back
Attending a conference or trade show
More responsibility
Public praise
Private praise
Letter to spouse
Gold star
Permission to delegate routine jobs
Corner office
Potted plant
Handshake from top-level executive
Mention in company newsletter
Special assignment
Flowers
New equipment
Choice of equipment
Choice of assignments
Choice of personnel
New desk
Inclusion in upper-level meeting
Party
Lunch with supervisor or owner

Think of how you would feel receiving any of the above nontangible reinforcements from your supervisor, especially the gold star. Applying these rewards at the right time, and in the right situation, reinforces the right behavior.

Chapter Summary

- Feedback is a motivational tool you can use to reinforce good behavior or change poor behavior.
- To be effective in giving feedback, learn how, when, and where to do it right.
- Once you've learned to use feedback to reinforce behavior, start giving tangible and nontangible rewards to recognize the *results* of that behavior.

Chapter 11
Moving Into Teams

■ The Purpose of Teams

The larger the organization, the greater the possibility that people will work at cross-purposes. You have already learned that to prevent this, a company needs to reorganize to get everyone going in the same direction and get production back on track. It's the top person's job to make the corporate vision clear, and to make sure everyone moves toward that vision. Reorganization consists first of identifying relationships critical to success, then defining success areas, setting goals, keeping score, and getting and giving feedback.

Is there more? What final or additional development can you take to anchor your shop securely in the future?

Teams! Teamwork gets everyone working together in thought, word, and action. What you have done by developing your people up to this point is to prepare everyone for teamwork. The preliminary work has been of great importance, but teamwork will keep your shop moving toward ever greater production and profit. As everyone in your shop becomes a member of a team, all members of your organization will become linked together, fulfilling the mission of your shop.

■ When to Form Teams

Forming teams is the final development toward corporate renewal. It is not the first step, but the last. A business can easily make the mistake of forming teams too early. It may form teams for the wrong reasons, such as to solve problems, or to get things going right when things appear to be going wrong. It's easy to say, "Let's try something new. We'll form teams!" But if people have not been prepared for this new venture, this new way of thinking and communicating, the teams will fail.

A sudden jump into a team environment won't work. Unless the groundwork has been laid—unless the entire organization is focused toward success—teams become an extra burden, another level of management that must be dealt with. Teams will only add to the confusion if they are formed at the wrong time or for the wrong reasons.

When you have implemented many of the ideas set forth previously in this book, you are ready to form teams. In effect, you have committed yourself to unleashing individual potential. You have opened doors to possibilities of working together more effectively by dissolving some of the traditional barriers that separate managers from workers, and workers from each other. Only when individuals are moving toward the expert level, with their goals personally identified and properly set, and everyone is receiving effective feedback, can teams begin to successfully plot the shop's course into the future.

▪ The Team as a Unit

Top teams are units of action. But usually a process of development takes place among team members before things work smoothly. Before a team can reach the point where it is a dynamic force, charting its own success, solving its own problems, and carrying the company into the future, each team member must undergo some changes. No one is exempt from this change process. Part of the change process is to begin to consider the team as a unit. This is done by putting team interests above individual interests. This is a hard lesson for some of us to learn, but an essential one if the team is to be 100% effective.

This does not mean that individual initiative or interests are subjugated by team interests. Individuals must be creative and must work smart for the team to succeed. What this means is that after the team makes a decision, everyone must support it, whether every team member agrees with the decision or not. If individual members of the team work against team decisions, the team and its ideas fail. It only takes one team member to destroy the work of the whole team.

That's why it's the responsibility of all team members to help forge the team into a unit. When team members work closely together, individual initiative and creativity are released. This occurs because people feel comfortable and safe, supported by their fellow team members, and they know that the team, as well as the company, recognizes and appreciates their efforts.

In most cases team members want to cooperate and help the team win. Team members also instinctively sympathize with the team leader or facilitator and rally to his side when difficulties between members arise. But, as important as the team leader is to keeping things under control, all team members must actively participate in the team's activities. For example, team members can exert peer pressure when others misbehave, thereby defusing most awkward situations. (Keep in mind that the team leader leads the whole team, not just the problem people or the outspoken people.)

It's not easy to work with others in teams. In fact, it often appears easier to work by oneself. We tend to idealize and romanticize the loner. But in truth it is cooperation and teamwork that have made people heroes throughout history. All great scientists, engineers, artists, and writers have had workshops, studios, publishers, or corporations behind them. Although inspiration may have struck an individual, that person was part of an organization or team that helped the individual turn inspiration into action into achievement.

Nothing is achieved in a vacuum. The more people realize that working together as a singular unit can help everyone achieve an element of greatness, the quicker the team becomes a top team.

■ Choosing the Team

Natural teams are the most effective teams. A natural team consists of individuals who naturally and normally work together. These individuals already have something immediate and specific to do together, and have already developed a relationship. They hold common views and objectives. For example, a natural team can consist of a supervisor and his direct subordinates, or the shop owner, the salesman, and perhaps the estimator.

Assigning your teams may be the most difficult thing you do. You will want your teams to succeed from the beginning, of course. Therefore, it is an important choice on your part as to which individuals will make up a team. If your company has a board of directors, you may want to discuss team formation with them, or discuss this with your shop foreman or others whose opinions you trust and frequently consider.

Everyone on the team must be vital to the team's membership. Don't put any "outside influences" on the team, as tempting as this may be. An outside influence is someone not working toward the same objective as the team. For example, there may be a tendency to add a company accountant to a manufacturing team, or a supervisor from another department just so he knows "what's going on." Don't do this. Keep the team pared down to essential personnel, otherwise it won't be effective.

Here's a good way to begin: Identify natural teams by examining the evolution of your business. When a business is just starting out, it is almost a team unto itself. Recall your business when you were just beginning. Perhaps you began the business in your garage, working alone. Next, you hired a machinist, then a machine operator. Eventually you had a full crew of five or six people working closely together, focused on the same results: getting orders into the shop and getting quality products out the door on schedule.

Perhaps your company continued to grow, each department becoming more specialized. You have marketing and sales people, production control specialists, estimators, planners, CNC programmers, machinists for setup, machine operators, and individuals in shipping and receiving. In a shop this large, you probably have several machinists, and maybe more than one person doing estimating and planning.

This is usually the point at which the shop runs into trouble. People begin working at cross-purposes, there is lots of tension and frustration, and there is very little interaction between departments. Machinists are upset because the programmer missed some detail on the drawing, or the programmer's approach to the job isn't what the machinist wants. The planner is upset because the estimator misjudged the labor hours involved in the project. With all this division among workers, where is the natural team?

Now think back again to those days your shop worked out of your garage. Who made up your team back then? Your team consisted of people possessing the following skills:

- sales
- estimating
- planning
- CNC programming
- machine setup
- machine operation

Teams whose members have these complementary skills are natural teams because:

- The association between the members is fundamental to the machine shop business. In a sense, the teams were formed when the shop started. And if the shop had to start all over again, individuals with these skills would be required.
- Their skills complement each other. They are dependent upon each others' skills.
- They are completely responsible for seeing an order through from beginning to end.
- When they are rewarded for continued success, they know the reward belongs equally to all of them. Every member had a hand in the team's success.

These skills and qualities are representative of a natural team. Another name for a natural team is a Qualified Manufacturing Team™, or QMT. Let's look at an example: Team A consists of five persons, each having one or more of the specialized skills listed above. You give Team A a job. They do their own estimating of labor hours, planning, CNC programming, and machining. They are even responsible for designing and building their own tooling. They hold themselves accountable for the quality work they do, and for getting the product out the door on schedule. They are aware of the critical relationships, and define success areas and set goals to monitor their progress. Because all members of a team have participated in the essential labor hour and planning process, they will fully support the effort when it comes time to produce the product.

Now, let's say you form Team B and Team C. Like Team A, each of these teams is also responsible for getting other orders up and out the door. It's up to them to do their own labor hour estimating, planning, etc.

There may be other ways to choose effective teams, depending upon the conditions of your shop and the type of work you do. However, always define your teams by complementary skills, not by individuals or specific tasks. Create teams where all the members naturally have the same, common goal. The extremely important communications of the unique details of every job is handled easily within this team structure.

If you have a team of engineers, a team of estimators, a team of planners, and a team of CNC programmers, you may be dividing your forces rather than bringing them together. Over departmentalization tends to limit communication and create distrust. The estimator team can easily blame the machinist team or the planner team if a job doesn't turn out right. Teams that are organized by department will fail because they lose sight of their critical relationships and don't receive the benefit of seeing the overall process.

■ The Benefits of Qualified Manufacturing Teams™ (QMTs)

Would it be easier for an individual, such as an estimator or planner, to involve himself with a *few* details of *all* the jobs that come through the shop? Would he miss any details? Or would it be more cost effective for a team with the required skills to attend to *all* the details of a *few* jobs? Would they be more successful? Naturally, the Qualified Manufacturing Team is better able to see projects through the entire production process.

A Qualified Manufacturing Team consists of individuals who have complementary skills—estimating, planning, tooling, CNC programming, machine setup, and operation. The QMT solves many of its own internal problems and job production issues because members are focused toward one result: getting a quality product out the door on schedule. The QMT has the authority and responsibility to make certain the job is done according to the standards of the shop (mission statement), and they hold themselves accountable for success.

Qualified Manufacturing Team members set individual and participative goals for themselves, and the QMT sets participative goals for the team. These goals are based on the QMT identifying its critical relationships and its areas of success. The QMT monitors its own progress toward its outstanding goal level, charts its trend line, and gives itself feedback on how it is doing or what it must do to achieve higher performance levels.

The Qualified Manufacturing Team offers additional benefits by:

- fostering innovative and creative solutions.
- defining quality standards.
- responding to customers' needs and wants.
- ensuring quality throughout, from inception to final product.
- focusing on company growth by viewing themselves as value added resources (VARs).
- turning errors into successful innovations.

By implementing QMTs you will find there is little need for direct supervision. QMTs take care of themselves by having a greater responsibility for the success of their jobs or projects. Accountability for labor hours estimated to labor hours actually taken is much easier to administer.

| **CASE STUDY** | Cedar Hills Machining is proud of its three Qualified Manufacturing Teams (QMTs), the Yellow Team, the Blue Team, and the Red Team. |

Darrell, a machining estimator with 15 years experience, was selected by the Management Team to be the captain of the Red Team. Pat, Tom, and Sandy, each with about five years of machining experience, were also assigned to the Red Team.

One of the Red Team's critical relationships was with Chuck Knolls, a first article inspector. Chuck performed dimensional inspections against drawings and work order requirements. Chuck and the Red Team had agreed to the following expectations, as shown in their chart:

EXPECTATION CHART

SUPPLIER	RECEIVER
Name: Red Team Position: QMT	Name: Chuck Knolls Position: First article inspector
List Expectations	List Expectations
Prompt inspection of the operation to minimize down time	Receive all drawings and documents with the first article part
Thoroughly review all documents for compliance	Part be free of oil, burrs, and chips
	Log the operation into the first article inspection log

Cedar Hills Machining had a long standing policy regarding inspection. This company policy stated that if the inspector accepted the part, that meant he would "buy off" the operation. The team was then authorized to continue with production. Without this "buy off," the team would have to make any necessary changes and submit another part to inspection. The purpose of the first article inspection was to prevent production errors, and therefore reduce scrap.

One morning, Darrell and Pat estimated and tooled a new job. They produced their first part of the production run. They cleaned the part thoroughly before giving it to Chuck for inspection, along with the part's documentation. Then they waited for Chuck's response.

Chuck returned the part to Darrell as quickly as he could, to minimize the Red Team's down time. He had "bought off" the part, so Darrell and Tom began production and produced 34 parts, just short of the team's satisfactory goal level.

Sandy and Pat worked the night shift. By the end of their shift, they had produced 37 parts, one part above the team's satisfactory level! Both were excited, knowing that they had a good chance of reaching their outstanding goal level, if they could keep their rejects low.

Before leaving, Sandy took a part randomly from the finished batch and examined it, just to assure herself there were no errors. As she inspected the part, she discovered that one of the true positioned holes was out of tolerance. After investigating further, Sandy determined that the wrong dimension had been programmed! That meant all 71 parts produced by the team were scrap!

When Darrell and Tom arrived the next morning, the team met to decide what to do. First, Sandy explained to the team how she had discovered the programming error that produced the wrong dimension. Sandy then produced the work order that showed that the part had been "bought off" by Chuck, the inspector.

"Therefore," Sandy concluded, "it's not our fault, even if Darrell did the programming. We had a legitimate go-ahead. Look. The work-order shows the part was bought off. Chuck should have caught the discrepancy. He should have noticed that the tolerance was off."

"I say we continue production, or else we'll get too far behind schedule" Pat said.

(cont.)

Tom disagreed. "Look, just because Chuck didn't catch the error on the first part inspection doesn't mean we should produce an order of worthless parts! Cedar Hills' motto is 'Quality is Service.' We're certainly not going to enhance the company's reputation if we produce junk."

Darrell insisted the team look at the problem from all angles. "We've got to decide how to solve this problem," Darrell said. "Then we've got to come up with a permanent solution."

Sandy agreed. "The term 'bought off' gives us a false sense of security. Operators believe that the responsibility for the quality of the part is transferred from them to the inspector at the moment the inspector affixes his stamp of approval to the work order. We've got to be more diligent. Anyone can make a mistake. If we're going to do quality work, we've got to initiate our own quality control. We've got to inspect our own parts."

The Red Team took these steps to remedy the problem. First, they programmed the proper dimension so Darrell and Tom could continue production. They knew it would be better to deliver the correct parts one day late than to deliver a whole shipment of bad parts on time.

Then the Red Team met with Chuck and Tony Barker, the plant supervisor. Darrell explained the problem to them.

"It's not wholly Chuck's fault," Darrell explained. "Since the teams are responsible for the quality of the part, and we have set goals to reduce scrap, we suggest that the first article inspection be considered only as 'another opinion.' It should not be called or considered a 'buy off.' The term is misleading. It makes people think that production can continue, when there still may be mistakes. We propose that the company make the teams responsible for double-checking the first article inspection. This puts the responsibility where it belongs—in the hands of the team."

Tony liked the idea so well he immediately brought it to the Management Team. The Management Team called a general meeting and announced the Red Team's suggestion. Tony complimented the Red Team's initiative and noted that the terms "bought off" or "buy off" would no longer be used. The first article inspection was to be a quality check and considered no more than "another opinion." The first article inspector would still inspect the part, but it was each team's responsibility to make certain that tolerances were correct.

QMTs provide a great place for training new people in the skills they will need to be successful in the trade. The QMT is also a perfect environment for a team member to start out as an amateur or nonprofessional and work his way up to expert. He soon may even become a team captain because he knows what a team is and how it works.

Incidentally, QMTs are a natural Advanced Quality System (AQS) team for those shops upgrading to ISO standards.

As your QMTs improve, so will your quality rating. As your QMTs progress, so will your customer base. As your QMTs succeed, so will your business. Be prepared to expand!

▪ Adding Other Teams

When a shop grows, it must increase administrative personnel to support smoothly functioning Qualified Manufacturing Teams. Your shop may add such personnel as accounting, which includes payroll, accounts payable, accounts receivable, and purchase orders. You may also add inventory control personnel, which includes shipping and receiving, as well as someone to manage overall inventory, from raw materials to finished goods.

Your shop may even grow at a rate that demands entirely new QMTs to be added! However, be certain that each team you form is vital to your shop. Each team must identify its critical relationships and success areas, then set three-level goals and measure its progress toward outstanding goal levels.

▪ The Executive Team

As shop manager, you don't *have* to be a team member on any of your QMTs, but it's probably a smart idea. You set the example by being a team member yourself, in addition to defining your own critical relationships in business, establishing your success areas, and setting your personal three-level goals. However, the key word here is "functioning." Only join a team

The executive team

if you are vital to the team's success because you offer one of the skills required.

If you are the shop owner or manager, you may want to form an executive team with your salesperson and supervisor. If you do, your team would work by the same rules and guidelines as any other team. The executive team would define its success areas, set team goals, and move forward. The one difference is this: as top person, you would be the leader of your team. It's your job to make certain everyone on your team can freely discuss thoughts and feelings.

■ Team Guidelines

Guidelines are vital to a team's success. You can either give teams guidelines, or have the teams meet and come up with their own guidelines at their first team meeting. Either way, guidelines clearly state rules and expectations, thereby uniting team members. Guidelines don't have to be elaborate or complex; a single page will do. Team guidelines *must* include:

1. A statement regarding the importance of full participation of all team members in team discussion and decision making. This statement can be followed by a list of ways to encourage the full participation of every member. For example, team leaders can go around the table and ask everyone's opinion on each issue. There can even be a rule in the guidelines stating that discussion stops if someone has to leave the room for any reason—even to go to the bathroom! Why have such a mundane rule? It emphasizes the importance of full participation of all team members. Will you hold a team meeting if a team member is absent? Make a decision on this and state this rule in the guidelines. The team must do all it can to confirm the importance of each team member's full participation and value to the team.
2. Guidelines must confirm that each team member is valued and all ideas are welcomed and accepted. The fear of having ideas rejected is what keeps many people from speaking up in a group. Thus, teams must strive to be nonjudgmental.
3. Hold the team meeting in a place conducive to discussion. The meeting place should be comfortable and reflect the importance of the team. If possible, hold the team meeting in neutral territory. For instance, don't use the supervisor's office. It's where

he hires and fires people. Instead, use a conference room if one is vacant, or a corner of the shop.

4. Choose a good time for the meeting, where there will be few or no interruptions. The team meeting should be short—in general, no more than forty minutes, or a maximum of an hour—to keep the meeting focused and brief.

Be sure to start on time whether everyone is present or not. Starting on time lets everyone know the meetings will always start on time. If the meeting starts late because the team is waiting for someone, this gives the message to others that they can come late because the team will wait for them. *This is the one exception to holding a team meeting without all members present.*

Remember, guidelines should be short and simple. Guidelines are a tool used to keep meetings focused and successful. Good guidelines help everyone leave the team meeting knowing ideas have been fully expressed and heard.

Guidelines aren't etched in stone. A team can always review its guidelines and make changes to them. Guidelines should be what the word implies—lines of guidance for the team, not hard-and-fast rules.

■ The Team's First Task

The first action a team must take, after it sets forth its guidelines, is to set goals for itself. It will measure its success by how close it comes to achieving its goals.

A team must set its goals in the same way team members set personal goals for themselves. The first thing the team must do is to identify its critical relationships. Following are a few suggested groups a team may wish to consider, based on the four categories of critical relationships:

- The executive team
- The management team
- Other Qualified Manufacturing Teams
- The employer
- The supervisor
- The external customers

- The external suppliers
- The co-worker or team that receives the team's output
- The co-worker or team that gives the team what it needs so it can do its work

After the team defines its critical relationships, it discusses how to succeed from the viewpoint of each critical relation. These are the team's success areas. Define these success areas in one word, if possible. Some common success areas are quality, accuracy, and timeliness of delivery. (For more information on success areas, refer to Chapter Six: Areas of Success.)

Individuals may wish to suggest some of the critical relationships and success areas they personally selected when they set their own goals. In some cases (but not all!), personal goals and team goals may be the same. But the team must make the final decision about which goals it wishes to set for itself.

After the team has defined areas of success, it can set tentative goals for itself. The team should have as few as possible. In many cases, six to ten is about right, but the team must decide. Remember, 30 goals are far too many. The goals should represent 80% of the team's responsibilities. Again, the team may adopt some of the goals individuals have set, or it may identify new ones. (Goal setting is covered in Chapter Seven: Using Success Areas to Set Goals.)

Some goals a team might consider are:
- Estimated labor hours / actual run
- # of minutes in team meetings
- # of scrap parts produced per shift
- # of work hours job is completed ahead of schedule
- # of minutes down time per shift
- # of parts produced per shift
- $ scrap value produced per shift

After the team has set tentative goals, it may wish to share them with the supervisor, or pass them along to the manager or management team for review and comments. When the team has received that feedback and is convinced the goals are appropriate and necessary to their success, the team can set three-level numerical goals for itself, using either the intuitive or statistical method, or both. (The team may find that it does not have enough data to set a statistical goal, particularly if it is a newly formed team. In this case, the team will have to set its minimum, satisfactory, and outstanding goal levels using the intuitive method.)

Once the team has set its numerical goals, it should appoint one of its team members as a scorekeeper or librarian to keep track of team goals. The scorekeeper can enter goal statistics into a computer if the company has an automated goal-tracking software package, or he can manually chart the team's progress toward its outstanding goal level.

The discussion the team goes through to identify and set its goals will be a valuable and memorable experience for team members. At each subsequent team meeting, the team should review its goals and trend line. If the goals address at least 80% of the team's activities—as they should—the goals will be sure indicators of what the team must do to achieve successful results.

▪ Team Goals and Personal Goals

Team members may already have defined personal goals before the company went to a "team-worthy" environment. Therefore, individuals have mapped out what they must do to succeed. They have defined critical relationships and success areas, and have set goals. And they are measuring their progress toward their outstanding goal levels.

Team members will find that when the team sets its goals, personal goals are synchronized with team goals. In most cases, the critical relationships will be the same for the team as for the individual, so some goals may be identical. Encourage individuals to keep working on both their personal and team goals, and to continue tracking progress. Working toward the team goals assures the success of personal goals. And when an individual succeeds, the team succeeds.

There may be rare cases where team goals and personal goals are not compatible. This is an unacceptable situation, because both the individual and the team will fail. If a team member feels this is the case, he can test his goal using the Five Goal Tests (on page 87). If his goal passes each test, there is no conflict. If any test raises questions about the goal, the team member can revise it or discard it, and focus on the rest of his personal and team goals.

■ The Customer Account Manager™ (CAM)

Although the Qualified Manufacturing Teams are responsible for all the manufacturing details of each team project, there ought to be one team member responsible for all the order processing details of those jobs. This unique position is called a Customer Account Manager™, and the person best suited for this position is the salesman. When you turn your salespeople into Customer Account Managers, you begin to promote a more natural flow of information.

A Customer Account Manager performs all the same functions your salesperson performs, including *personalizing* your shop in your customer's eyes. When you personalize your shop's relationship with your customer, it leaves a lasting impression. When a customer receives an immediate and accurate response from the one person he has met in your organization—the CAM/salesman—you put yourself way ahead of the competition. Your customer will not forget your attentiveness to the details of his job. His word-of-mouth alone enhances your reputation. And this occurs because one person, your CAM, has built a quality *relationship* with the customer.

A Customer Account Manager is responsible for all order processing details, as well as the scheduling and material purchasing aspects, of each job he sells. Therefore, some of the Customer Account Manager's success areas may include:

- entering a sales order into the system
- scheduling on a master schedule
- purchasing material in coordination with other CAMs

The main purpose of the Customer Account Manager is to attend to the details of the jobs he brings into the shop rather than leaving those details to others. The CAM should be a QMT member, so he knows each job's status every step of the way. If there is any problem with the job, at any stage of its production, the CAM is aware of the problem and, if need be, he can inform the customer.

A Customer Account Manager would also be a candidate for membership on either the executive team or a management team consisting of QMT captains. CAMs might also be members of a CAM team. The CAM team defines its critical relationships and success areas, and selects numerical goals, just as any other team. It may include the following success areas:

- sales
- customer relations, including telephone and correspondence
- contract negotiation
- customer follow-up
- labor hour quotes to QMTs
- dollar quotes to customer
- review of QMT schedules

The benefit of converting a salesperson into a CAM is that each team now has a direct link to its most important critical relation: the shop's customer. The CAM and the production people will share the responsibility for the orders. Because the CAM will be relaying the customer's needs directly to the production people, they will associate each order with a valued customer. The shop will be able to keep better track of all jobs, and should a problem occur, the CAM will be in direct communication with the customer. This makes the customer more comfortable because he knows and trusts the CAM already. (For more information on CAMs and QMTs within the production process, see the Appendix.)

CAMs will make your shop truly customer-driven!

▪ Linking Teams Within the Shop

Although each team may be autonomous in the sense of being responsible for carrying out a job and pursuing its own team goals, all teams within a company must work together to effectively carry out the corporate mission. Teams must also communicate with one another regarding production logistics, such as equipment access or scheduling. Otherwise, the shop may have the same problem it had between individuals—an expectation/performance imbalance and teams working at cross-purposes.

One way to assure that teams work together is to link the teams into a network. This can be done very simply. After you have formed natural teams, and each team has defined its own goals and is moving forward, consider ways of bringing various team members together for the purposes of review, evaluation, and management.

Here's an example. Described in the chart are three production teams, A, B, and C. Each team consists of four team members. The person at the top of each column is the team leader: Barry, Mary, and Gary.

Team A	Team B	Team C
Barry	Mary	Gary
Ellen	Bruce	Steve
Eduardo	Johnny	Louis
Bernard	Mike	Gretchen

These three teams are linked to the management team as illustrated in the following diagram:

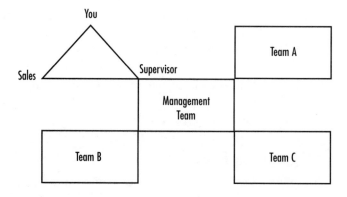

Your team—the executive team—consists of you, your lead salesperson, and your supervisor. The executive team is represented as a triangle in the diagram.

The management team consists of your supervisor (we'll call him Larry) and the team leaders from teams A, B, and C: Barry, Mary, and Gary. It is the central rectangle that connects the executive team to all other teams.

Larry is a member of the executive team, and he is also team leader of the management team. Barry, Mary, and Gary are members of the management team, and they are also team leaders of their respective production teams.

Therefore, you can see how easy it is for the supervisor, Larry, to share executive decisions, such as forthcoming contracts and major events, policy shifts, and expansion plans, with the management team. The management team members can, in turn, share this knowledge with their respective production teams, which can then shift their focus or plans to accommodate executive decisions. When the management team meets, it will discuss where the company is going, where it is now, and what changes may need to be addressed.

Linking teams as shown in the above example enables a free flow of information up and down company lines, and helps push management down to the lowest level. Linked teams also minimize the levels of management in a shop, which is good. The fewer levels of management there are, the fewer barriers exist between people.

Administrative teams can be linked to the executive team in the same way QMTs are linked. For example, one member of the executive team can be the accountant. However, since accounting is a specialized department with distinct functions, you may want to keep accounting personnel separate from other teams, perhaps in a special administrative team. The important thing is to maintain the natural flow of information and operations between management and those on the front line.

▪ Competition Among Teams

You don't want teams to compete the way sports teams compete because all teams should be working toward the same goal—the success of the company. The whole purpose of teams is twofold: to get everyone going in the same direction, which increases production (and therefore profit), and to create a sense of unity (where people comment that the shop is a nice place to work). This environment nurtures amateurs into experts, attracts new experts, and creates company pride.

When the goals or achievements of one team are held in front of the other teams like a carrot before a horse, you run the risk of fostering competition between teams that may result adversely on the company. Teams that compete against each other often go to great lengths to win, resulting in disillusionment, anger, and a refusal to participate.

Of course, there are instances where friendly competition can be exciting and fun, but these types of activities must be carefully introduced. A healthy competition is present when each team strives to reach its own goals and directs its competitive spirit toward the marketplace to win over accounts from other machine shops through quality production, timeliness of service, or better price.

CASE STUDY   The vice-president of a large, well-known, international blue-chip company was always on the lookout for new ways to inspire his sales teams. These salespeople were top-notch, all of them pulling in six figure incomes. The company had offered expensive vacation packages to its winning sales teams, as well as automobiles, club memberships, and electronic equipment. But the vice-president was running out of ideas.

One day the vice-president's second-grade son announced at the dinner table that he had won a gold star for getting all his homework in on time for the week. He proudly showed the gold star to his father and mother, and the gold star was prominently hung on the refrigerator door.

This gave the vice-president an idea.

On the following day the vice-president put a poster in the executive cafeteria, which was on the 37th floor in the corporate headquarters. The poster had the name of each sales team on it. After lunch the vice-president announced that the team that attained its goal of new customers who would place orders within the next three months would receive a gold star.

The vice-president later commented that sales increased rapidly as teams worked at top speed to reach their goal and earn a gold star! The teams made it a game. They weren't competing against each other for expensive gifts or fabulous vacations—they were working for a simple gold star! And the competition was healthy because it was directed outward, toward the marketplace. All of the teams provided a tangible benefit to the entire company—increased sales.

The point to this anecdote is this: nothing is too immature or sophisticated to consider when encouraging teams. The "game playing" aspects you can introduce work well with teams. Just be sure everyone accepts the challenges, that the incentives are within good taste, and that you don't foster unjust competition between teams.

▪ Team Feedback

A team, like an individual, needs feedback. Feedback—positive, negative, and neutral—can be given to the team the same way it's given to an individual. Feedback can be given formally by the shop's executive team members at team meetings, of course, but another way to give effective feedback is to meet informally with the team. Briefly tell the team how it's been doing. When speaking to a team, it's critical that you speak to the *whole* team. Don't leave anyone out, and don't single anyone out. You don't want to give the impression that one or two people on the team are better performers or more important than others, and they're the ones receiving your praise. You might even want to ask each team member to express his opinion on how the goal was achieved. This is information you can then share with other teams, or at your executive team meeting.

Teams respond well to poster-size feedback, such as graphs or other visual aids. These are frequently better than oral statements because they speak directly to the whole team and can be viewed over time. They are trophies of accomplishment.

▪ Team Rewards

In addition to reinforcing the results of individuals, you will want to reinforce the team as a whole for good performance. Even a simple comment such as "Your team cut production costs by 5% over the last time" recognizes the specific results of the team's efforts.

Consider giving rewards to a team for the following results:

- ▪ A positive trend line three weeks in a row
- ▪ Not falling below the satisfactory goal level
- ▪ Attaining the outstanding goal level
- ▪ Good cooperation between team members

Consider these ways to reinforce teams for good work:

a gold star
cash bonus
lunch with owner
plaque
team presentation to other teams
team presentation to board of directors or executive team
day off with pay for team members
profit sharing on successful job
gift certificates to a fancy restaurant
jacket or tee shirt with the company name on it
company party in honor of the team
flowers and candy for each team member to give to spouses
a day of your time spent working with the team
on the team's project
two tickets to each team member for a sporting event

When giving rewards to team members, keep in mind that the reward should have some value, reflect the team's good performance, be useful, inspire pride, suit individual taste, and reflect the company's image.

■ Why Teams Fail

A team must be vital to the operation of the company or the team will fail. Don't form a team as an afterthought. The team's existence must be related to the corporate mission.

A team is different than a task force. A team is long-range, with management responsibilities including the power to execute its own decisions. It has a secure place in the corporate picture. When in place, it should be considered permanent. A task force is a temporary group of people given one task to perform or one problem to solve. As soon as the task is accomplished, the task force disbands. Don't make the mistake of giving your teams one-shot jobs, and don't make task forces permanent.

When teams fail, it's frequently for one or more of these five reasons:

1. Lack of team guidelines. No one taught the team how to operate as a team.

2. No goals. The team doesn't know what it's really supposed to be doing.
3. Poor or inappropriate feedback. No one tells the team it's on the right track, or if the team should make changes and *get* on the right track.
4. No reinforcement (or the wrong reinforcement). The team does not get rewards or recognition for doing what it thinks is a good job.
5. Lack of team leadership. No one sets the example.

Just like individual employees, teams need training, tools, and the proper equipment to be successful. Teams also require motivation and reinforcement. Without proper support a team may work at cross-purposes with other teams, or in opposition to individual initiative.

Here's the secret: treat a team as an individual. Care for it by nurturing it toward the expert level. Use all the same techniques with the team as you would with an individual—sharing the vision, reinforcement, rewards, problem solving, identification of critical relationships and success areas, establishment of goals, and feedback.

CASE STUDY   Aero Machining Technologies, Inc. is a high-tech aircraft job shop. When the local large airplane manufacturer received some new orders, Aero was rewarded several large contracts. Anticipating the new work these contracts would bring, Aero management decided to go to a teamwork environment.

Gary Smith, Aero's acting CEO, decided to form teams by departments. He created a machinists team, a quality control team, a CNC programmers team, an estimators team, and so forth. Then Gary and Mike Carr, the plant supervisor, set numerical goals for each team.

Aero immediately ran into many problems.

When the machinists team met, they developed a long list of complaints about the estimators. The estimators team spent their meeting time complaining about how slow and uncooperative the machinists were.

"Where are your solutions?" Mike Carr, the plant supervisor asked one team captain.

(cont.)

"What solutions?" The team captain answered. "These are the problems we see, and we expect something to be done about them."

Mike reported another problem to Gary. Two of the teams had decided not to meet. When Mike asked a team captain why his team wasn't meeting, the team leader responded, "Why should we meet? There's nothing to do. A meeting is a waste of time. We're not going to achieve the goals given to us, and no one does anything about the complaints we forwarded to Gary. We just want to do our jobs and collect our paychecks."

Gary called in a consultant. He explained to the consultant, "I want my people to work in teams, to work together. I know that teamwork will move my company into the future. However, creating teams has caused more problems and confusion. I don't know where to go from here. I don't know how to fix the present problems."

After looking over the team structures, and taking a walk through the shop, the consultant knew exactly what the problems were, but things had gone almost too far to fix. The failure of the teams had convinced many people that teamwork may be a management ideal, but in reality was a disaster. They wanted nothing to do with anything that had the word "team" in it.

The consultant explained to Gary, "We have to start over from the beginning. First, dissolve the teams. Just let people do their work. After we initiate a program of employee support and turn things around, we'll begin team training. This training will consist of identifying critical relations and defining success areas. When this is accomplished, we'll devise a system where employees will create expectation lists. This will help people learn what is expected of them by those who give them the work they have to do, and by those whom they send their work to."

"Will this interfere with our production?" Gary asked. "We have contracts and work orders."

"Not at all," the consultant replied. "In fact, the more work the company has, the more clearly your employees will see the value to what we're going to accomplish."

"When do we form the new teams?" Gary asked.

"When everything else is accomplished and your employees are prepared to try again. And when we do form teams, they

(cont.)

will be done vertically—that is, they will be Qualified Manu-facturing Teams. The teams will be made up of people from different departments who work together, rather than people who work in the same department. Each team will be respon-sible for estimating, planning, and producing their own parts. They will have a lot of autonomy because they will know ex-actly what they have to do to succeed.

"After teams are formed, we will supply each team with care-ful guidelines. They will decide what to discuss at each team meeting. We will supply them with agendas and train them how to modify these agendas to meet their specific team re-quirements. We will also train all team members in team lead-ership. Everyone on a team must have leadership skills, or the team won't fully function.

"And last, after the teams have successful team meetings and begin to solve problems and reach their team goals, you have to decide how you are going to reward your teams.

"After these failed teams are disbanded, we'll begin the pro-cess that will make each QMT, and therefore each individual, a success at what he does."

Chapter Summary

- Forming teams is the ultimate step to creating a top shop; employees must be prepared to form teams in order for the teams to be successful.
- A natural team—called a Qualified Manufacturing Team—should consist of individuals having complementary skills and sharing a unified objective.
- A QMT should establish critical relationships, define success areas, and set goals in the same way that individual employees do.
- The executive team and the QMTs in your shop can be linked together by the formation of a management team.
- Just like individuals, teams require feedback, reinforcement, and rewards in order to achieve goals and be successful.

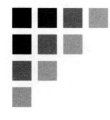

Chapter 12
Communication Skills for Team Leaders and Team Members

■ The Importance of Team Leadership

To be successful, a team must have strong leadership, and no team task is as critical as good leadership during a team meeting. The team leader can make or break a team meeting. To be effective, the team leader must convey certain attitudes during team meetings, such as encouraging everyone to speak, ensuring people take turns, and being courteous when another expresses himself. A team's leader keeps discussion on track and flowing toward the single point under discussion.

A team leader is an equal member of the team. The team leader's opinion is equal to everyone else's opinion. Therefore, the leader must facilitate the team process without imposing his own opinions!

Encouraging participation is the hardest part of being a successful team leader. At first team members may be uncomfortable speaking their minds in front of their coworkers. However, as they learn to trust each other and as they gain identity as a team, they will express themselves more freely.

■ Leading Successful Team Meetings

Here are "Four Simple Truths of Team Meetings." Team leaders may wish to print these "truths" at the top of each team meeting agenda to remind people of the importance of participation.

The Four Simple Truths of Team Meetings

Truth #1: Meetings go well when everyone talks.
Truth #2: Meetings fail to be productive when no one wants to speak.
Truth #3: Meetings are boring when few dominate.
Truth #4: Meetings are chaotic when there are no rules.

Following are simple rules for team meeting leadership that work. Train your shop's team leaders to take these actions to assure successful meetings:

1. State and restate the topic under discussion so that everyone knows exactly what's being discussed. Restate the topic because everyone listens differently. Some of us must hear things several times before we know what's being talked about.

2. To stimulate and encourage discussion, ask open-ended questions. An open-ended question is a question that cannot be answered with a yes or a no. Open-ended questions usually begin with "How do you feel about...?" or "What is your opinion about...?"

3. Phrase questions in a positive way. For example, ask, "What have you observed that would help us be more efficient?" instead of "Why aren't we more efficient?"

4. Encourage quiet team members to participate by asking direct questions to those who don't volunteer. But then be appreciative and receptive to their statements to encourage continued participation. Remember, every team member is vital to the team.

5. Keep quiet after asking a question. Allow a team member at least 15 seconds to respond to the question before jumping in again. Many people need time to compose their thoughts. Don't feel it's necessary to fill up silence with talk.

6. Use body language. Nod, smile, and make eye contact with team members. This is very important. *Always look at the person who is speaking!* Don't fiddle with papers or the agenda when someone is talking. The team leader's attention lets the speaker know he is listening and sets the ex-

ample for the rest of the team. Also, make frequent eye-contact with everyone on the team to recognize their presence.

7. Rephrase ideas or questions if there's no response the first time around, but elaborate only briefly. Rephrase responses or comments people make if it seems a team member may not have clearly understood what was said, or if what was said is confusing. Rephrasing is a simple way to help everyone understand what's going on, and to encourage participation.

8. Write down, or have someone write down, every idea mentioned. It's always a good idea to have someone take notes. That way, if the team gets off track, the leader can always ask the note-taker to repeat the last item under discussion.

9. Use people's names! Everyone loves to hear his name. Calling on a person by name makes the meeting personal, immediate, and friendly.

10. Speak when it's your turn. As a team member, the leader certainly has the right to speak, but should try to do so in the order the team establishes. Being team meeting leader does not require a comment on everything that's said.

11. Don't put anyone down for saying something unusual. Sometimes wild ideas give insight into how to solve a complex problem.

Inviting Guests to Meetings

A team or team leader should never ask someone who is not a member of the team to "sit in" on a team meeting. The reason is this: an outsider will disrupt the team's actions, and probably thwart the team's efforts. If it is a successful team, it has defined its success areas and set its own goals. It has already established and cemented relationships among its members. It doesn't need an outside person "viewing" its activities. However, a team can always hold a special meeting in which the team and another person can discuss issues.

■ The Six Point Agenda

Each team meeting must have an agenda. There are always two main parts for the agenda:

1. Goals
2. A few other items of interest to team members

Team goals *must* be the first part on the agenda.

The team should designate one of its members to put the agenda together prior to each meeting. That member can be the team leader, if the team selects the leader to do this. Any team member can contribute an item to the second part of the agenda, but these items should be added in advance. Agenda items should not be added at the team meeting, or the meeting will go on too long or fall apart into useless talk.

The person who prepares the agenda is also the one who keeps a copy of the agenda on file after the meeting. That person should fill out the "team's copy" of the agenda, three-hole punch it, and keep it in a three-ringed binder.

The agenda preparer should distribute the agenda—and related materials—to each team member prior to the meeting or at the beginning of the meeting. For example, when meeting to discuss a new job and estimate the labor hours for it, the team captain should supply drawings and other information to be distributed to each of the team members in advance so everyone is prepared to discuss the job.

Below is a model for team meeting agendas called the Six Point Agenda. These six questions should make up the first part of every agenda, and therefore, the first part of each team meeting. These agenda items constitute the heart of the team's meeting because they address the most important action for which the team is responsible.

Six Point Agenda

Date:
Time beginning:
Time adjourned:
Place:
Team members present:

Part I—Team Goals

1. What factors are causing recent positive trends?
2. Who deserves praise?
3. What factors are causing recent negative trends?
4. What are we going to do about negative trends? What's our plan of action?
5. Are we dealing with "can't do," "won't do," or "can't be done" problems?
6. What are we going to do to solve problems?

Part II—Additional Items

The Six Point Agenda should be used by every team, including executive and management teams, to examine each of the team's goals. If a team has 10 goals, apply these questions to each of the 10 goals. After each team goal has been discussed in the context of these six questions, the team can certainly discuss a few items of its own. Part II of the Six Point Agenda is for additional topics of discussion requested by team members, such as laying out new jobs.

The agenda must not be controlled by any one person or by the company. The team requires autonomy in which to work. Any type of restraint limits the team's creativity, its ability to make its own decisions, and ultimately, its responsibility for the outcome of its production. Thus, the agenda must belong to the team. The items on the agenda *must* be important to the team.

This means that the shop manager shouldn't tell the team that it only has a half-hour to work through the agenda. It's up to the team to make these decisions.

■ Learning to Use Leadership Skills

Facilitating a meeting can be a difficult situation, thus the facilitator must be trained to use leadership skills in team meetings. Here are some questions and answers team facilitators may have about dealing with certain kinds of problems that can arise at a team meeting.

Question	Answer
What do I do when someone makes snide remarks, attacks another team member, or takes subtle digs at others' comments?	Don't let him get away with it! Ask pointed questions that bring his hostile remarks to the surface. It will cause him to back down. Ask others in the room if they feel the same way about things. Let the team gain his cooperation through communication. Peer pressure helps defuse the situation.
What do I do when someone loses his temper, uses abusive language, or throws a temper tantrum?	Give him a few moments to vent his feelings. Then interrupt—get into the conversation! Get his attention by standing up. Make eye contact and forcefully make a statement without arguing. Say to the team something like, "Ed has every right to make that comment. It's as valid as any of yours." But take his objection seriously, and look for the reasons behind his behavior, even if it was inappropriate.
What do I do when someone insists he is right and won't listen to anyone else?	Listen carefully to what he says and rephrase the major points he makes. Then, if you have accurate and up-to-date evidence that supports other ideas, share them with the team. Ask for feedback from him and for the opinions of others. Thank him for his opinion, and respectfully ask him to be quiet if he continues to push his point. Don't get him mad by being a know-it-all yourself.

(cont.)

What do I do when a person just isn't very smart, or doesn't know much about the subject under discussion?	Not all of us are smart. An expert is smart about one subject, but may be ill-informed on many other subjects. Invite opinions from everyone. If someone makes a comment about a subject he doesn't know much about, give him a way out. Help him along by filling in the gaps he may leave in his statements. And remind team members that they can use team meetings for their own education.

The facilitator's job, just as it is every team member's job, is to make the team discussion run smoothly. After all, team members are all on the same side. In the beginning, provide training and instruction to new team members in how to brainstorm, withhold judgment, and give constructive criticism. As the team develops, it will become a unit, and team members will come to depend upon each other. They will recognize and appreciate the strengths and weaknesses in each other, and learn to use those differences to benefit the team.

▪ Personality Types on Teams

All team members, and especially team leaders, must realize that everyone will have to learn to accept and communicate with their fellow team members. It would take another book to describe all the personality types a person meets on a team, and this section doesn't attempt to do that. Just know that many people have different expectations and views, and certain ways of addressing and handling problems, and they use these "skills" they've developed over the years to solve problems. These skills and behavioral styles work for them, or a person wouldn't continue using them. There's nothing right or wrong about any of these "personality types" and the way they solve problems.

As team members get used to each other they become more aware of how other team members' minds work. This can be a good education for all team members, because team members can adopt problem-solving skills they haven't tried before.

The following list identifies some types of team members. These personality types, and the problem-solving skills and types of power they use, are common among people at all employment levels.

Personality Type	Typical Behavior	Advantage	Disadvantage
The Giver	Uses control over something another person wants or values, such as a raise or bonus. The Giver likes to give and get rewards.	Fast acting and positive	A person may work only to the degree necessary to receive a specific reward.
The Coercer	Likes to withhold something of value, or remove something already pos-sessed, to gain cooperation. The Coercer likes to punish others when they make mistakes.	Immediately gets the message across	Creates bad feelings. If a person has something, taking it away or threatening to take it way causes anger.

(cont.)

Personality Type	Typical Behavior	Advantage	Disadvantage
The Legitimizer	Respects the power of position. When a person has the "supervisor" title, the title bestows legitimate power and everyone accepts it. The Legitimizer is keenly aware of who the boss is, who controls the paycheck.	Legitimacy lasts as long as the title lasts.	Respect is only given to those in powerful positions. Respect diminishes if the title holder makes unwise decisions.
The Expert	Wants people to admire his knowledge and ability. Experts have proven track records and experience.	Long-lasting. Once an expert, always an expert.	It takes time to establish expertise in others' eyes. You can't just tell people you're an expert. You have to prove it.
The Likable Guy	Wants to like and be liked by everyone.	When people like you, they won't let you down. It's usually easier to work with this type.	It takes time to establish "likability," and maybe not everyone will end up liking the Likable Guy.

(cont.)

Personality Type	Typical Behavior	Advantage	Disadvantage
The Name-Dropper	Who he knows is the issue.	It's fun to drop names, and gives the impression—real or imagined—that the Name-Dropper is part of a "super network."	Others may not be impressed. The name dropped may be unknown, unacceptable, or both. The Name-Dropper places more value on who he knows than what he knows.
The Director	Likes to tell others what to do and how to do it	Focuses on the issue	Can cut others out of the consultative process. Usually has trouble relinquishing control in team settings.

Everyone has a different personality and style. No one should try to be someone or something he's not. People see right through that. When on a team, individuals can be successful by being themselves and working to make the team a unit.

■ Dealing with Difficult People

Teamwork forces us to work together. This means we may have to discuss ideas with people whose values or personalities are very different from our own. In most cases, this benefits us. We learn from the viewpoints and attitudes of others.

But not everyone is easy to work with. It only takes one person to disrupt the team's progress, rendering the team ineffective. It can become a discouraging chore to serve on the team with a difficult person.

Some symptoms of personality conflicts include:

- Team members wanting to avoid meetings
- Negative trend lines persisting
- The team losing motivation
- The team failing to come up with action plans to achieve its goals

Usually such problems can be traced to one individual with whom the team members are having difficulties.

There are a few things you can do to help your team leaders and members learn to work through difficult situations.

1. Encourage members to commit to learning to work *with* the difficult person and accepting him just as he is. Also encourage them to decide in advance how to deal with the difficult person.
2. Difficult people often have good ideas. Suggest that team members look for the positive ideas from the difficult person.
3. Instruct teams to take a break after someone has created tension in a team meeting. Break for coffee. The team leader can take the difficult person aside and talk to him privately. Confront him. Tell him in point-blank terms the problem the team's having with him. Ask him to come up with a solution. Suggest that he help get things back on track.

It takes time and effort before each team member respects each other team member and everyone appreciates the differences in styles and personalities.

CASE STUDY Mirror Machine Works had just finished its management training—implementing the support, reinforcement, and problem solving that gave employees confidence and focus. It had taken six months for the owners to turn this failing shop around and focus it toward success, and today MMW is a contender in the market. Due to being a shop that now has a reputation for working hard and working smart, top machinists from other shops were submitting applications to MMW. They wanted to be part of the present success and future growth at MMW.

(cont.)

Mirror Machine Works was co-owned and operated by Stephen Jackson and his sister, Jenny Newcombe. Stephen and Jenny worked with a few long-time employees to come up with a good company slogan:

Machining Excellence and Dependability

This slogan said it all about their company mission. Machining excellence and dependability is what each of their customers were looking for.

Stephen and Jenny decided to start teams up one at a time. They chose Jerry, one of their newest machinists, to be the team captain since he'd worked in a team environment before. One afternoon they met with Jerry to give him all the forms his team would need to get started. Then they asked him to set up the first team meeting.

"There's one thing we'd like you to do at your first team meeting," Stephen said. "We want your team to identify a team mission statement."

Jerry thought about this a moment and was about to protest. The company already had a mission statement. Why would the team need a separate one?

Jenny seemed to read his mind. "It serves several purposes," she added. "First, it helps communication. It gives everyone something to talk about. Being an abstraction, there are no right or wrong decisions to make. It helps team members get to know each other a little. And second, it will help them focus on our company mission—Machining Excellence and Dependability."

The next day the first QMT at Mirror Machine Works met in the small conference room at 9:00 a.m. Jerry looked around the table at his new teammates. There was Jim, an old-time machinist who had worked in about every shop in the area over the last thirty years. Larry was perhaps the most inexperienced member on the new team. He'd had about five years' experience running CNC equipment. Billy was a nice, friendly guy—a good operator who always seemed happy doing just what he was doing.

Jerry told everyone to pour some coffee. "Our first order of business," he said, "is to come up with a team slogan."

"A what?" Larry asked.

(cont.)

"Slogan," Jim clarified. "You know, something that says something about us. Something we believe in and can be proud of as a team."

"We've already got a slogan," Larry protested. "Machining Excellence and Dependability."

"What do you think about it?" Jerry asked.

Larry shrugged. "Okay, I guess."

"What about you, Jim?"

"Okay."

"Billy?"

Billy just grinned and shrugged.

Jerry realized that the discussion was not progressing as he had hoped. Despite his teammates' discomfort and reluctance to participate, he decided to keep the conversation going. "It's a good slogan," he said. "It tells us what is most important."

"It's fundamental," Jim agreed. "I mean, every machine shop must produce quality parts. Otherwise, we lose our customers. If there isn't a customer, we're out of a job."

"Right," Jerry said. "And if you keep quality and cost in mind during the whole production process, you're going to know your customer and keep your customer happy."

Now this comment suddenly got Billy fired up. "How can we get to know our customer? I'm a machine operator, not a salesman. I don't even know who the customer is!"

The discussion continued for some time. Team dynamics began to take place as everyone got caught up in the discussion. First Jim, then Billy caught the spirit of the exercise. Larry, however, didn't seem willing to participate much. He grumbled and argued, always bringing up reasons why a newly suggested team slogan was stupid or wrong in some way.

Finally Jerry asked Larry, "We've all made suggestions. It's your turn, Larry. We're not going back to work until we come up with our team slogan. Tell us which of the ideas you like best."

Larry mentioned he would want to serve on a team that was reliable and dependable. "Something the customer can count on."

Billy recognized that comment as the team's solution. "That's it! The Team the Customer Can Count On."

Sometimes a person doesn't know he is being difficult. He may, for instance, consider his constant interruptions a way to get at the truth of an issue. It may not occur to him that his constant questioning is annoying. Or a person may be a nit-picker, unable or unwilling to ever see the larger picture or visualize where the team's discussion is going. Each time an idea is brought up, the person may pick at unnecessary details and imagine countless ways the idea won't work.

Another difficulty is the team member who always talks about the way things were done at his previous place of employment. He may say, for example, "This is the way we did it at Evergreen Manufacturing." And he may make some good points. The problem arises when a person insists that the way things were done at the place of previous employment is really the best way, and everyone else is off track.

In the process of forming teams, some previously hidden problems may become glaring. These usually have to do with uncooperative people. A supervisor might even ask himself, "Why didn't I see this problem before?" The difference is that a person's uncooperativeness is more apparent on a team than it is when individuals work solely for one manager or supervisor. A person can "hide" in a company, just producing enough to get by, when a company does not have a team environment. A person cannot hide when he is a member of a team. Unfortunately, if a team member is a chronic hardship to the team, that member is also a hardship on the company.

There are always going to be loud people, articulate people, quiet people, smart people, etc. on the same team. Team members must recognize these differences. A good team leader can actually capitalize on these differences, as long as he makes certain everyone participates in the team discussion. But it's ultimately up to the team leader to handle difficult people before tempers flare and control is lost.

If the team is unable to deal with the difficult person, upper management must step in and solve the problem. But managers should not develop an employee throw-away policy. While it may seem easier to just get rid of the difficult people rather than develop ways to correct the problem, this usually becomes the start of a high employee turnover rate.

The solution is to accept people just as they are, and help all team members learn to appreciate their differences and communicate effectively. Remember that team building and team action is a new experience to many. In one sense each team is running its own business within the confines of the larger enterprise. The team has a right to expect and receive cooperation. To be successful, the team must draw on the creativity and natural intelligence of all its members.

■ Sabotaging Success

Although most people are anxious to be successful, there may be a few who want everything to fail. They don't want their company to succeed. Maybe it's because they're afraid of the demands success will bring to their jobs. A person intimidated by success usually works to encourage failure, and may spread rumors about impending doom.

Sometimes a long-time employee can become the team's difficulty. When an old-time employee refuses to accept change and attempts to sabotage success, it's usually because he's in love with the old business, the old way of doing things. He may have sacrificed during the company's salad days, foregoing paychecks or putting in long hours, just to see the business succeed. He wants everything to revert to the "good old days."

As the manager, it's up to you to make the old-timer understand that the "good old days" are gone. In fact, a cursory review of those times reveals that the business was innovative and up-to-date then, otherwise it wouldn't have survived, but now the company's lost its edge! Remind the long-time employee that the purpose of current changes the company is undergoing—those changes which culminate in forming successful teams—is to get the company up-to-date again. To be competitive a business must challenge and be challenged by innovative management and state-of-the-art operations.

Another example is the supervisor who is not used to success. He can easily become a barrier to his company's success. He can feel intimidated, and may fear that everyone will be successful but him. He may imagine that when the shop's owner sees he's not successful, he will be fired.

When a team member attempts to discourage success, someone with authority must talk to him. This can be the team leader, shop owner, or supervisor. Take him to a neutral place, such as out to lunch. Attempt to pinpoint the real reason for his anxiety or apprehension. When you find the reason, assure him of his value to the company. Use gentle persuasion and reassurance to get him on the "winning side."

Occasionally this can't be done. There may be no way to win over a person who is determined to sabotage success. When this occurs, and you have exhausted every avenue to help him accept the changes that are coming, there are only two solutions.

The first is to give him a lesser or special position in the company where he can't influence others. Of course this lets him know right away that his worst fears are being realized—he's being pushed out of the mainstream. But explain to him why you are taking these steps. Tell him that you can't have him working against the program everyone else is working to accept. It's not fair to others, and it's not fair to him. There's a chance, admittedly slim, that he may change his attitude. But remember, you don't have a lot of time to spend on one person convincing him to play ball with the rest of the team. You have a business to run.

The second solution is to let him go. You should take several steps before you let an employee go to prevent difficulties later on.

First, document your preliminary discussions with the employee. Before you meet with the employee, outline on a piece of paper what you are going to discuss. After you have addressed each issue on your outline, have the employee sign and date the document. This offers proof that you have attempted to work with the employee, and that you have addressed each of the problem areas. He cannot later say that he was unaware a problem existed and no one gave him a chance to correct his mistakes.

If the employee still presents a problem, interview him again. This time, tell him that he will be let go if he doesn't change specific behavior. Again, outline what you are going to say before your meeting with him and have him sign and date the warning notice. This accomplishes two things: it lets him know he will be fired if he doesn't change specific behavior, and it protects you. It lets everyone know that the employee was fully and fairly warned.

If the employee still does not make the changes you outlined, call him into your office to dismiss him. Don't fire him on the shop floor, or in front of others.

Firing a person is never easy. In some cases it may have negative repercussions throughout the company. People might think, "If they let him go, who's next?" On the other hand, employees may be relieved to learn that an uncooperative person, or one who refused to pull his weight, has been let go.

Just remember, firing an employee is expensive. The company loses all the training and experience invested in the person. If someone is hired to replace the fired person, there is hiring and training expense involved in bringing the replacement up to speed. And there is always the uncertainty of whether the new person will "work out."

Firing a person should always be the last resort. But one way or another, you must deal with the problem. Don't ignore it. One person can demoralize an entire company.

CASE STUDY   Take the case of David Markoff, a first article inspector at Arlington Machining Technologies. David had been with the company for some time, but was never an easy person to get along with. He was a good inspector, but sometimes insulted people when they asked him a question.

When Arlington began training their employees toward goal-setting standards, offering reinforcement and guidance, David was the last person to cooperate. He reluctantly participated in filling out his Expectation List, and offered insincere expectations with information no one could use, such as "just give me good parts."

Spike Stanton, the plant supervisor, tried to bring David on board. He found himself going back to David with an already-filled out expectation list and helping him fill it out correctly with information David's suppliers—those whose parts he inspected—could use so they would do a better job.

"Just write down that you want the drawings and work-order requirements to accompany the part," Spike said.

(cont.)

David frequently made negative statements about a machinist's performance behind the machinist's back. Spike confronted David about this on more than one occasion.

"I can't have this, Dave," Spike said. "You can talk about the article you're inspecting, but don't say anything personal about the machinist, no matter what your opinion is. If you have a real complaint about someone, bring it to me. Don't spread it around the shop."

Things got worse. One machinist even threatened to quit if David didn't stop badmouthing him and others in the shop.

Spike didn't want to fire David. He was really a good inspector. But he couldn't have him criticizing the machinists behind their backs. Arlington Machining could not move forward if this type of behavior persisted.

Spike wrote down the following:

David Markoff:
Too many complaints that you criticize machinists behind their backs.
Bring all criticisms of individuals to me, Spike Stanton.

Date:_____
Signed: _____

Spike took David into his small office, just off the shop floor. He showed him the paper and asked if he had any questions.

"Well, the machinists could do better work," David muttered.

"That's not the point," Spike said. "Besides, that's my problem, not yours. Your job is to inspect the parts. That's all. And your comments are starting to affect the other inspectors. I don't want a shop where it's 'us against them.' I want a shop where we work together."

Spike had David sign the report. Spike said, "I'm going to keep this report in your file. I hope this is the last I hear of this."

Unfortunately, it wasn't the last of the problem.

Spike heard other comments. The two other inspectors were starting to make similar criticisms, and Spike knew they were being coached, however indirectly, by David.

Spike called David into his office one more time. This time, he told David that he would be dismissed if he didn't stop backbiting. It was demoralizing the whole shop, and infecting the

(cont.)

other inspectors. Spike had David sign another paper that said he would be dismissed if he, Spike, heard any more complaints from the machinists.

A week later, Spike was forced to let David go. To Spike's surprise, the whole shop seemed relieved, including the other inspectors.

■ Motivating the Team

What motivates a team? Reaching its goal. However, your company can provide incentives and encouragement along the way, such as:

- A trophy or plaque, a long-lasting reminder of success.
- Giving praise, such as, "This team is great. You are one of the company's most important assets."
- Planting a tree in honor of the team.
- Making a donation, on behalf of the team, to a favorite charity.
- Holding a cake and ice cream party to celebrate an accomplishment.
- Asking a winning team to do something special as a group, such as going to a customer's business to look over a project and getting to know the customer better.
- Letting the team choose a work assignment.
- Buying subscriptions to magazines for each team member.
- Giving each team a bulletin board where it can post anything it wants: memos, jokes, news articles, cartoons.
- Giving caps, tee-shirts, jackets, coffee mugs—anything with a logo is appreciated.
- Inviting the shop owner to sit in on a special team meeting.
- Taking Polaroid photos of winning team members at their workstations, and putting the photos up for everyone to see.
- Talking about success areas and goals, which emphasize their importance to everyone.

Train your shop's team leaders and members well, then unleash them by giving them the authority, autonomy, and accountability they need to be successful.

Chapter Summary

- The team leader's job is to facilitate meetings, which means encouraging all members to participate and keeping the discussion focused.
- Teams should follow the Six-Point Agenda to keep meetings on track, flowing, and relevant.
- The greatest challenge team members face is learning to respect each others' differences and to communicate effectively, but it can be done through practice and training.

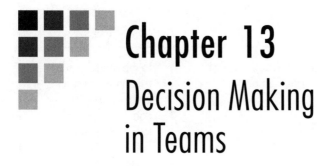

Chapter 13
Decision Making in Teams

■ The Making of a Top Team

The most important function of a team is coming to a mutual team decision. The thought process team members invest in reaching decisions, and the ongoing relationship development between team members, make decision making easier as individuals become accustomed to working together as a team.

But making decisions is just the beginning. Carrying out the decisions is what the team is all about. The results of each decision—how quickly and thoroughly the team turns a team decision into action—is what makes a top team.

■ The Three Types of Decisions

There are three types of decisions: command, consultative, and participatory. The type of decision made depends on who is making the decision and under what circumstances. The following chart explains these scenarios in greater detail.

Decision Type	Definition	Example
Command	A decision made by one person.	• In the military, for the most part, decisions are made by higher command and given to lower personnel. For instance, during a battle no one wants decisions made by committee or a team. Decisions must be made spontaneously and authoritatively. • If someone runs into the room and yells, "Fire! Everyone run!," this is a command decision. Loss of life results if a team has to meet to decide where to run or how fast to run.
Consultative	A decision made by one person after listening to the opinions of others.	• A supervisor discusses a project with several machinists, then decides how to implement the project plan. • After hearing pros and cons about a new sales campaign, a vice-president in charge of sales can make an informed decision.

(cont.)

Decision Type	Definition	Example
Participatory	A decision made by a team.	• The team meets and decides how to lay out a project, and how it should be scheduled. • A problem among team members arises, or a problem in the company occurs. The team takes up the issue on its agenda and solves the problem.

There are good things about each type of decision. The command decision is the most common and popular type of decision used today. Even in a small machine shop that is team driven, there may be instances when the shop's top person needs to take immediate action on a particular decision. You might tell a team to stop their progress toward a specific goal and solve an emergency that has come up.

The consultative decision is common in larger businesses, especially in fields of marketing where many ideas must be sifted through, or a marketing analysis made, before a product can be effectively introduced.

The participatory decision—the team decision—has one great advantage over the command or consultative decisions: the team members immediately understand the decision and support it. No one has to be instructed as to the thinking behind the decision and why it should be implemented. There is no lag time necessary to implement the decision because it's not a decision coming from the top down.

All types of decisions are necessary given certain situations. But as much as possible, let teams make participatory decisions regarding shop goals. Use consultative decisions when setting company policy and direction. Reserve the command decision for emergencies.

▪ How to Reach a Participatory Decision

A team is a decision-making body. A true participatory decision requires everyone on the team to equally participate in reaching a decision.

There are three methods a team can use to reach a participatory decision: majority, plurality, and consensus.

Decision-making Method	Definition	Drawback
Majority	A majority is when more than half of the team members agree to support a decision. A majority is usually confirmed by taking a formal vote, either written or oral.	The problem with majority votes is that some team members may remain dissatisfied. ("I didn't vote for this stupid idea. I voted against it!")
Plurality	A plurality occurs when *most* of the team members present at a team meeting support a decision. Reaching a decision by plurality vote is usually done to facilitate action when all team members cannot be present. Plurality voting is similar to majority voting.	It has the same pitfalls as majority, but in addition, reaching decisions by plurality vote or agreement can easily foster the problem of people saying, "I wasn't even at the meeting when this stupid idea was decided!"

(cont.)

Decision-making Method	Definition	Drawback
Consensus	Consensus means endorsement for the course of action. Consensus does not necessarily mean 100% agreement among team members that a particular solution is the best one. It means *all* team members are willing to give one possible solution a try.	None

■ How to Reach a Consensus

A top team strives to reach decisions through consensus. It's not only up to the team facilitator, or team leader, to move the team toward a consensus. Every team member must "agree to disagree" on occasion while still working at reaching a consensus.

When attempting to reach a consensus on a team decision, document the activity. The team facilitator or another team member should write everything down so everyone can see. The team can use a chalk board, white board, or large newsprint pad. Writing things down helps people concentrate on what's being discussed, confirms that everyone's idea is under consideration, and accurately expresses what the team member said.

Train your teams, especially the team leaders, to take these steps to reach consensus:

1. Write down the topic under discussion. For example, if the team is discussing a negative trend line and what to do about it, write down the goal under discussion.
2. Each time a team member offers an opinion or suggests a solution to a problem, write the team member's comment on the board.

3. After each idea is expressed and written on the board, restate it. Have the team member confirm it's correct.
4. Continue asking for ideas until the team (or facilitator, if the team gives the facilitator this responsibility) feels that there are enough ideas.
5. Ask the team to choose the best ideas on the board and circle the best phrases. Take the best ideas, and condense and combine them into a new decision. Write the combined idea in as complete a form as possible.
6. Ask if everyone is willing to support the course of action as expressed by the combined idea. If everyone is in agreement, consensus has been reached.
7. If *anyone* on the team is confused by the wording of the idea, restate the idea in a different way. Again, if everyone is willing to support the idea after changes are made, consensus has been reached.
8. If *anyone* on the team disagrees with what was written or refuses to support the idea, or even a part of it, request alternative ideas or decisions. Write them on the board. List all ideas under discussion without hesitation. Everyone must have the opportunity to express his view. Let everyone explain which part of the idea he disagrees with and why.
9. If people are confused and nothing seems to be clear, analyze the decision-in-progress. Draw a line down the middle of the blackboard. Ask for a list of advantages and disadvantages regarding the topic of discussion. Write advantages to the left side of the line and disadvantages on the right.
10. Continue answering objections and refining the idea until consensus is reached.

Don't be in a hurry to reach a decision. The thought processes that go into the dynamic of decision making are as important as the decision itself.

If the decision reached or idea chosen by the team later turns out to be wrong, it's okay. The team can always have another meeting and change its plan of action. The important thing is not whether the decision is right or wrong. The important thing is that the team believes it's chosen the best possible solution at this time, and everyone agrees to support it.

CASE STUDY   A team at MicroTech Machinery was comprised of some veterans and novices. The good news was that the novices could learn from the veterans, and thereby increase their efficiency and hence their value to the company. The bad news was that the novices often introduced ideas and plans the old-timers knew wouldn't work. The two novices on the five member team often felt overlooked or ignored when the team made decisions.

The team was involved in developing a manufacturing plan to produce cable quadrants. One of the more inexperienced machinists, Denny, had specific ideas about setting up the procedure, and Lewis, a veteran, constantly disagreed with him. At one meeting, Lewis and Denny got into a heated argument that degenerated into insignificant details.

Nell, the team captain, had an idea. She knew that many of the points each of them made were vital to the plan, while other points were insignificant in the long run. "Let's approach it this way," she advised, bringing their argument to a halt. "Let me write all the ideas on the whiteboard. Then we'll pick the best ideas."

This pleased Denny, who felt the team never took his ideas seriously.

Lewis and the other veteran offered their ideas first, then Denny stated his plan, and the other novice on the team added hers, as well. Nell entered her idea, also. They went around the room three times, taking turns, each time modifying, changing, or adding to the manufacturing plan.

The team finally settled on a plan. Lewis and the other experienced machinist, Mike, weren't too happy with the plan, because it didn't fully take into consideration certain raw materials inventory and other details that could possibly arise. But they agreed that the overall plan was solid.

Denny and the other novice were pleased to see their ideas incorporated into part of the plan.

Although they didn't know it at the time, the team had taken a giant step toward their own development and identity as a team. From that point on, Denny never argued with Lewis or Mike, but listened carefully when they spoke. He began to "hear" some of the experience behind their statements.

In fact, as the team continued to develop, Lewis gradually took Denny under his wing, teaching him many skills he had learned through experience.

(cont.)

In the end, the plan the team had chosen wasn't the best, but it did incorporate everyone's ideas and it did get the job done. Denny and the other inexperienced team member saw what Lewis and Mike had been talking about as the job unfolded. The veterans, on the other hand, realized that some leeway could be given to accommodate the inexperience of the younger team members. Mostly, they all discovered that changes can always be made in a plan to bring it into line. No plan is written in stone.

■ The Art of Brainstorming

Brainstorming is a term given to the free flowing of ideas without restraint. It is highly effective when a team is looking for *new* ideas or trying to break through conventional patterns of thinking to solve a problem. A team leader should not suggest brainstorming techniques if general discussion is moving along smoothly. Consensus can be reached through good discussion. Teams should only use brainstorming to break new ground, or when a decision can't be reached and the team seems to be at an impasse.

There are two styles of brainstorming:

1. Round Robin: Start with one person and go around the room. Each team member takes a turn tossing out an idea. If a person does not want to speak, he passes to the next person.
2. Free flow: Team members toss out ideas at random; there are no rules of order.

Whatever style of brainstorming the team chooses, the team leader should make certain that the flow of ideas remains focused. The team leader must also know when to draw the flow of ideas to a halt so the team can begin to shape the best ideas into a decision, usually in the second or third round of ideas. When heads begin nodding in agreement, it is probably time to stop the ideas and start looking for consensus.

The following are useful guidelines for brainstorming:

1. Define the topic under discussion or write it on a board so everyone can easily see it. This will keep the team focused.
2. Maximize quantity. The goal is to generate as many ideas as possible, so keep asking for more.
3. Wild ideas are welcome! Ask for creativity and imagination.

4. *Never* criticize an idea or the person making it, and don't let anyone else be critical. Don't judge ideas during brainstorming; accept *anything!*
5. Don't discuss ideas as they come up, just list them.
6. Build on and combine ideas.
7. It's okay not to have an idea.
8. Record or write down all the ideas quickly so everyone can see them. When writing down ideas, spelling and grammar don't count. Abbreviate when possible. Write down duplicate or similar ideas without comment.
9. Don't number ideas. Numbers imply one idea may be better than another because it's closer to the top of the list. Also, people begin associating ideas with numbers. It's better to say, "I like the idea about moving inventory next to the shipping area," rather than, "I like idea number 12."
10. When writing down ideas, don't stop at the end of the page. Immediately flip the page and continue. The end of the page doesn't mean the end of ideas.

▪ Implementing Team Decisions

How quickly and effectively a team turns its decision into action is what makes a top team. Even as the team members leave their team meeting, each member should be thinking of his part in the action plan.

Here are some tips that help a team turn a plan into quick, decisive action:

- Be certain of the goal. Don't leave the team meeting until everyone knows exactly what the team is doing.
- Keep all plans as simple as possible. Don't make things complicated.
- Constantly and frequently communicate with one another.
- Focus all resources on a single target—the team goal. Then translate all resources into action.
- Remove all obstacles. If something hinders the team's action plan, find out what it is and why it's hindering the team and remove the obstacle.
- Make sure every task moves the team closer toward its goal.

- Carry out exactly what the team requested.
- Get it done. Teams must follow through on their plans.

A top team, comprised of experts, begins carrying out team decisions even before the team members hit the shop floor.

Chapter Summary

- There are three types of decisions: command (best for emergencies), consultative (best for setting company policy), and participatory (best for setting shop goals and solving problems).
- Teams should work at reaching participatory decisions that all team members agree to support (called reaching a consensus).
- Teams should practice brainstorming when they need fresh ideas on handling tough decisions.
- Teams should act quickly and decisively after forming a plan.

Chapter 14
Lead Your Shop to the Top

■ The Anatomy of a Top Shop

Your relationship with your shop is never static. It is either getting better, or it's falling apart. Never assume that your healthy, stable relationships with those who work for you will continue indefinitely. Don't think that your customers will always be your customers. Complacency is a dangerous thing.

Consider the large corporations in America today. Look at how many of them rested on their laurels after attaining preeminence in their field, only to be surpassed by younger, hungrier, more aggressive small companies who streamlined their work force and grabbed the action.

What you did yesterday, what you successfully achieved, is past history. History can delude you into thinking you're on top, and that you'll always be there. But, the bright side is that you can learn from the past and use that experience to make things better. No one has had the experiences you have had.

To move boldly into the future:

1. Focus on your business. Find out where you are, who you are, and what you are doing.
2. Master your job. Become an expert, a leader. Demonstrate those qualities of character you want to see in those who work for you.

3. Develop your company. Once you have mastered what you do, you can innovate.

■ The Permanent Solution

To turn a machine shop around isn't done in one step. There isn't a set of rules that can be followed in sequence. No one can promise and deliver perfect solutions. It takes creativity, intuition, and hard work to move a business from its present level into a successful future. It takes the same qualities and dedication—facing the same fear of the unknown—it took when you started or took over the shop.

There are lots of quick fixes available for any ailing machine shop, such as training seminars, inspirational meetings, clever shortcuts, focus groups, encounter groups, and assorted activities for top executives and their subordinates. Many of these work well to some extent, but none are permanent. Usually, these meetings deal only in generalities and never address the specifics necessary to solve problems. Most businesses tire of paying employees to attend expensive and glamorous meetings that don't deliver permanent and positive change.

Few, if any, ideas presented in seminars increase individual performance and keep that performance going. What's needed is a plan that works. The plan must be intrinsic to the business. It must be a natural next step forward. It cannot be something superimposed on your business.

The plan works best if it's built in from the beginning. This way, the plan makes sense to all those who participate in it, from salesman to machinist. It is part of everyone's history, the "corporate culture" that brought everyone together in the first place. But don't despair if your shop didn't have a plan from the start. It's never too late for you to work with your employees in making changes and turning your shop into a Top Shop.

Here is how to turn your shop into a Top Shop.

Part 1—Individuals

1. Know who you are. Take time to define your vision. Where are you going? What do you want from your business? Do you want a business that runs by itself so you can go on extended vacations? Do you want a shop that can compete with

the best shops in town? Do you want a reputation others hold in awe? Develop a mission for your company. You can often define your mission in a slogan, or phrase, that encapsulates what you are all about. And think about your overall corporate goal. Then think about how you are going to set goals to complete your strategy.

2. Begin the change process by preparing yourself to handle all reaction to change. Remember, you're going to implement a plan that will change the course of your future and affect the lives of those who work for you. There will be some resistance, but there will also be support. Prepare to coach everyone through the change process.

3. Focus everyone on his task. Offer support. Reinforce good behavior and good results. Help people succeed by giving them the tools, materials, equipment, and attention they need, and by being a leader. Avoid mediocrity, get focused, treat others with dignity, listen, and learn the good news and bad news about how things are going. This is how you can make informed decisions.

4. Each employee, including the top person, must identify critical relations in the workplace. Who is responsible to whom? Who gives you the work you need so you can do your job? Who do you give your work to so they can do their jobs? Have everyone fill out the Expectation List so they know who expects what from them and what to expect from others.

5. Help everyone succeed by determining how to meet the expectations on their Expectation Lists. These expectations are their success areas, areas of action they must focus on if they are to succeed in business.

6. Set three-level numerical goals based on these areas of success. Set goals either privately or in participation with others—especially with your "customer" and "supplier." Select either a statistical or intuitive goal-setting method. Once an individual sets his numerical goal he can begin tracking the results, either on computer software or a printed chart. Make changes and solve problems based on the goal's trend—whether it moves toward the minimum, satisfactory, or outstanding goal level. Test each goal with the Five Goal Tests: the Mission Test, the Balance Test, the Uniqueness Test, the Push-Down Test, and the 80% Test.

7. Identify amateurs, nonprofessionals, professionals, and experts. Keep amateurs moving toward the expert level by eliminating problems, and keep experts on top by offering encouragement. Amateurs need lots of guidance—they don't know what they don't know. Nonprofessionals begin to see what they don't know, so they are eager to learn. Professionals can easily make a living at what they're doing, but they can't yet put all the parts together. Experts are the mentors, the trainers, the teachers. When you have no doubt a person can perform a task, that person is an expert.

8. Reinforce good behavior. Let people know what behavior and results you expect by giving feedback—information they can use.

9. Discourage negative behavior. Stop actions that are harmful. Harmful actions keep the individual from reaching his goal, and they interfere with others. Solve problems so each employee experiences success.

10. Ignore what is unimportant. Don't spend time on the insignificant, the idiosyncratic, or the eccentric. Don't try to change people. Create an environment where people can change themselves.

11. Give tangible and nontangible rewards for reaching goals and having positive trend lines. Reward the results that people achieve as they move upward toward the expert level.

12. When your shop has turned around, each employee is focused on his task. Each employee knows who is critical to him, and what he has to do to succeed in the eyes of those critical relations. Each employee has identified and set numerical goals. Each employee has tested his goals and knows that by attaining them, he has succeeded in his own eyes, from the viewpoint of his critical relations, and in your eyes.

Part 2—Qualified Manufacturing Teams

13. Prepare your salesmen to become Customer Account Managers (CAMs). The CAM is responsible for the job he sold from beginning to end—from the initial contact to the delivery of the finished product. He must work closely with his QMT so he knows the status of a job at every moment.

14. Identify your teams and decide who will serve on them.
    - Qualified Manufacturing Team—Individuals who exemplify complementary skills: operator, machinist, estimator, CNC programmer.
    - Management Team—The supervisor and team captains from each of the QMTs. The Management Team allocates equipment for jobs and coordinates general shop procedures.
    - Executive Team—The owner and two or three others, perhaps a supervisor, salesmen, accountant, or office manager. The Executive Team moves the shop toward the future.
15. Train and educate QMT members. Give each team suggested guidelines, the Six Point Agenda, the corporate mission statement, Expectation Lists, scorecards, and any other information the team might need to do its work.
16. Review with each team the three types of decisions, how to reach a participatory decision, how to reach a consensus, the art of brainstorming, guidelines for brainstorming, team leadership skills, basic problem-solving skills, how to create team unity, and how to maintain team diversity.
17. Have each team identify its critical relations, define success areas, and develop its Expectation List for each critical relation. Have the team begin completing its scorecards—setting numerical goals based on their areas of success (the expectations of their critical relations). Some common critical relations are the executive team, the management team, other QMTs, the employer, the supervisor, the inspectors, the persons or teams who give the team the parts they need to do their work, and those to whom the team gives its finished product.
18. Have QMTs chart their progress by entering all critical relations, success areas, and goals into a tracking software or printed chart.
19. Then unleash your employees' potential by giving the QMTs the responsibility and authority to plan a job and see it through to the end.
20. Motivate and reward your teams just as you motivate and reward individuals. Give each team feedback—information the team can use to become a Top Team.

▪ The Consultant Option

You may be considering hiring a consultant to achieve top performance from your people. But before you do, there are some things you should know.

There are two types of consultants: operational and management. An operational consultant offers specific information about how to operate one aspect of business, such as finance, inventory, contract negotiation, equipment, or production. A management consultant helps a business owner or manager increase performance by getting the most out of everyone from top-level to front-line people. Both types of consultants have one goal: to increase profit or save the company money.

What a consultant does is find the strengths and weaknesses of your business and define some of the barriers you face. He can make a diagnosis that may redefine the problems, and he provides recommendations for you to consider. Often he can do this better than you can because he can easily drift among departments and talk to employees at all levels of the operation. This extra freedom allows the consultant to take a step back and view the company from an objective perspective. This viewpoint, accompanied by the consultant's experience and knowledge, can often be a source of valuable information for a harried shop owner. Ideally, the training and coaching a consultant offers energizes people to become star performers.

Finally, the management consultant should not be looked upon as an outsider interfering with your business. In order for a consultant's work to be effective, it must be done with complete support from top management.

▪ The Consultant Problem

There are three major problems to face when hiring a consultant.

The first is cost. Can a small business, say a business of 10 or fewer people, afford to hire a consultant? Hiring a consultant often costs more than his fee. When a consultant has finished offering training and coaching, will the company make a profit using the consultant's advice? This is the true cost of a consultant—the value of his effect on the shop.

The second thing to consider is whether the consultant has the necessary expertise in the specific area you're hoping to improve. If he can only speak in generalities about complex areas you need help in, then you probably won't receive any usable advice. For instance, hiring a consultant with a background in finance to solve shop management problems can be very costly and may not produce results. It is very important in the job shop industry that the consultant has "been there, done that."

The third thing to consider is whether you will follow the consultant's advice. If a business won't follow the consultant's advice—for whatever reason—there's no point in hiring one! This isn't necessarily a reflection on the consultant's work. It's just that hiring someone for his advice and not taking it is an obvious waste of time and money.

The solution is to hire the right consultant, and only if you plan to take advantage of his expertise. Hire someone you know will get the job done. A good rule of thumb is to hire a consultant you personally like, one you have rapport with and can easily talk to. Spend time discussing your situation and his background before signing any contract.

Remember, the consultant works for you, just as your attorney or accountant works for you. He must prove his worth by getting results.

▪ The Shop of the Future

There was an era when the machine shop's owner was the most skilled machinist in the shop, but this is no longer true. With the current rise of communication and technology, the technician of today possesses multiple skills. We have each become experts; sometimes our expertise overlaps the experiences of others, sometimes not. A bright shop manager will hire individuals who far exceed his abilities in certain aspects of the trade.

The economy of the entire world is also in a state of change. The world has become interdependent, and every nation relies heavily on others for economic and political stability. This, of course, makes each of us more dependent upon a global economy, rather than the ups and downs of business in our backyard. This new economy, fueled by the explosion of science and technology, brings home to everyone one important question: What's going to happen to me?

Machine shops can either become lost in the maelstrom of over-whelming events, as has been described in some bleak modern novels, or can take charge, using modern technology for their benefit.

Progressive management addresses this issue, eagerly anticipating and incorporating the changes and chances of both technology and the global economy. A smart manager knows that workers no longer blindly follow rules they had no part in defining. He creates a better shop, a work environment that responds to certain human needs common to all of us. He creates a shop that strives for excellence in production and values, knowing that he will attract and keep the best workers by doing so. And he realizes the necessity of paying employees fairly for their high-level skills.

Following are some characteristics of the future shop owner. Many of these characteristics have always held true, while others specifically address the challenges of our time.

- Be a strong, effective leader. A leader is one who sets the example by unleashing the potential of others.
- Don't wait for things to happen to you. Be proactive and make things happen your way. To be proactive is to be in control.
- Challenge yourself. Don't avoid tough issues, difficult decisions, or confrontations.
- Do new work, not old work. It's easy to give lip service to something new or innovative, without taking action on it. It's easy to rest in a comfortable environment, doing the same day-to-day work, even if that environment is going downhill.
- Accept the responsibility for coaching and guiding employees toward success. They may not understand what you are doing at first because no employer has ever helped them in this way. But when they catch on, they will join you in striving for excellence.
- Be slow to see mistakes. Be quick to respond to inflexibility and to "cop-like" attitudes.
- Make sure supervisors, including yourself, are role models for change.
- Think in terms of ground-breaking performance.
- Support those people who have unique ideas. Foster creativity as long as the person is producing results. Excellent machinists are creative, innovative, clever people.

- Victories are always small. Sometimes we overlook them. Two people formerly at odds with each other who can now work together is a victory. Many small victories make success inevitable. Recognize victories—yours and your employees'.
- Be emotional. Be thrilled. Agonize over failed schedules. Be impatient with continual failure. Let people know what you expect. They will interpret your more passionate responses as their areas of success and take action to fulfill your expectations.

The time is right for the visionary shop manager to initiate a goal-setting program that reflects values. The field is open for the smart shop manager to attract the best people. You cannot build a strong organization by holding people back. Build on what they know instead. When you do this you set into motion a series of events that moves your shop swiftly past your competitors and confidently into the future.

Appendix

Job shop operations are very complex, especially if there are customer materials and traceability requirements. The smooth flow of information through a shop is critical to its success.

The following are step-by-step descriptions of two types of job shop organization: the more traditional, departmentalized job shop operation and the team-based Top Shop! By comparing them, you will see the many advantages to implementing the changes required to turn your traditional shop into a successful Top Shop.

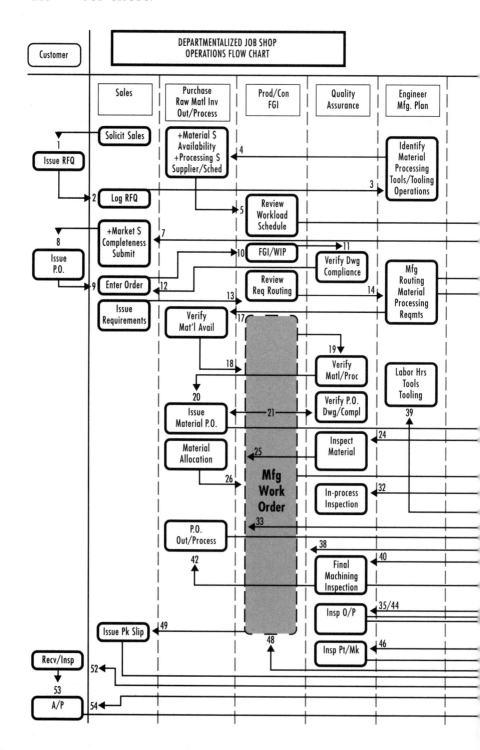

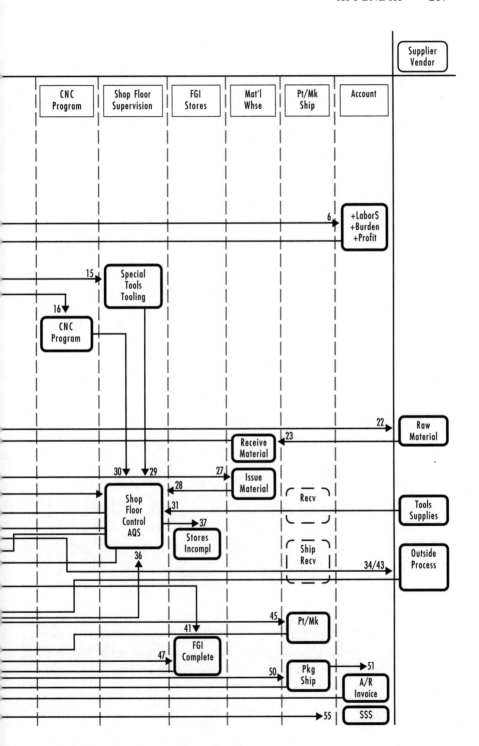

Departmentalized Job Shop Operations Flow Chart

| Sales |

Sales—Your salesperson solicits sales from existing and new customers.

| Issue Request For Quote |

(1) Customer—The customer issues a Request For Quote (RFQ) to the salesperson. This document is typically accompanied by drawings and other specifications.

| Log RFQ |

(2) Sales—The RFQ is logged into the system to track the quote and assure that the quote is submitted back to the customer on time. A check is made with finished goods inventory (FGI) to determine if the parts have been manufactured in the past.

| Identify Material Processing Tools/Tooling Operations Labor Hr. |

(3) Engineering—Upon receipt of the RFQ from the sales department, the engineering department identifies all material requirements, any outside processing needed, tools and tooling, operation requirements, and labor or machine hours associated with those requirements.

Responsibility/Accountability—By separating the hours from the dollars within the quoting process, each department involved can then monitor and improve estimating procedures. Once an order has been received, entered into the system, planned, scheduled, and run, the actual labor hours required to run the job and the tools or tooling expenses can then be compared to the estimate. This greatly increases the accuracy of future estimates and fine-tunes your job scheduling methods.

| +Material $ Availabilty +Processing $ Supplier/Sched. |

(4) Purchasing—Upon receipt of the RFQ from the engineering department, the purchasing department obtains quotes from suppliers for all material and outside processing, tools and tooling, and special requirements as identified by the engineering department. Material availability is also checked and noted on the RFQ.

Responsibility/Accountability—Obtain the lowest price possible from the supplier. High prices only make your quote higher, thereby resulting in lost work. It is important that the person who actually buys the material from a supplier is the same person who obtains the quote! If the person who solicits quotes is not the actual buyer, the supplier is likely to quote a higher price. He would quote a more accurate price if the person soliciting the quote is the actual buyer.

(5) Production Control/FGI—Upon receipt of the RFQ from the purchasing department, the production control department reviews the estimated labor and machine hours, the estimated material, and processing lead times. Production control notes on the RFQ any scheduling considerations that may be relevant to the customer's requested delivery schedule.

> Review Workload Schedule

Responsibility/Accountability—Maintaining an accurate production schedule is the heart of a good manufacturing operation. Promising the customer delivery dates that are unreal or not obtainable just to get the work will eventually anger the customer and result in a decrease of work.

(6) Accounting—The accounting department adds dollar amounts to the RFQ based on work centers used and the estimated labor hours. Work center and labor rates are developed by unique formulas designed to reveal *actual* costs incurred in manufacturing. A burden is added to the RFQ to cover all overhead expenses, and profit is added separately, only once. It is common for shops to add a percentage or dollar increase to individual items, such as material and out-

> +Labor $
> +Burden
> +Profit

side processing. For example, some shops have a policy where they charge material to the customer at their cost plus 20%.

This may confuse your quoting process. It's very important to develop and list *actual* costs on your quote form. In this way the salesman knows what it's actually going to cost the company to manufacture the parts. In conversation with the customer, he then has the opportunity to negotiate the price, while ensuring that the company can still make money.

Responsibility/Accountability—The accounting department is responsible for the development of actual labor hours, burden, and profit. It is important these rates be accurate.

(7) Sales—The salesman adds any additional dollar amounts to the bid based on what he thinks he can get for the job. After checking the quote for completeness, he submits the quote to the customer.

Responsibility/Accountability—The salesman is responsible for giving a fair and competitive price. The salesman is answerable to the customer for the price, the quality of the product, and the agreed-upon delivery date.

(8) Customer—Once all issues are resolved, the customer issues a purchase order. The purchase order includes quantities, delivery dates, and any special instructions to the company.

(9) Sales—Upon receipt of the purchase order, the salesman enters all necessary data into the computer or whatever system is provided, including quantities, delivery dates, and any special instructions. Should there be any future changes to the order, the sales department is responsible for making those changes in the system.

+Market $
Completeness
Submit

Issue P.O.

Enter Order

FGI WIP

(10) Production Control/FGI—A check is made on the status of work in process (WIP) and finished goods inventory (FGI) for the part number ordered to determine if the part has been made in the past. If so, any unsold parts are identified and sent to quality assurance.

Verify
Dwg Compl

(11) Quality Assurance—Any unsold FGI parts are routed to quality assurance to be inspected for compliance with the current order requirements, including drawing and special purchase order instructions.

Issue
Requirements

(12) Sales—Upon the completion of the FGI status check, the *total quantity of parts to be manufactured* is determined and then issued, along with the shipping requirements, to the production control department.

Review Reqmt's
Request
Routing/Info

(13) Production Control—A review of the shipping requirements is reviewed and a current routing, complete with material and processing requirements, is requested from the engineering department.

Mfg Routing
with Material
Process Reqmts

(14) Engineering/Mfg. Plan—Engineering develops an accurate and complete manufacturing routing. This includes all material and processing, as well as all operational requirements complete with setup and runtime standards.

Special Tools
Tooling

(15) Shop Floor/Supervision—Shop floor personnel are notified of any special tools and tooling that will be required for the job. A tooling work order is issued for the purpose of tracking labor and materials costs of tooling built in-house.

CNC Program

(16) CNC Programming—The CNC programming department is notified of any programming requirements. Required programs are created or updated and made ready for shop floor personnel.

Verify
Material
Availability

(17) Purchasing—Material and outside processing availability are verified with the suppliers for scheduling considerations. Even though availability was noted at the time of quoting, it is a good idea to obtain an update at this time because conditions change at the suppliers.

Create
PROPOSED
Work Order

(18) Production Control—Upon receipt of the routing, material, and processing requirements, *run quantities* are determined and a manufacturing work order is created. The work order contains all the necessary information pertaining to material and processing requirements, including the quantity of parts to be manufactured, a manufacturing start date, and manufacturing operations.

Verify
Material
Processing

(19) Quality Assurance—Upon receipt of the work order, the quality assurance department verifies that the material and processing noted on the work order are in compliance with the customer's drawings, documents, and purchase order. It is important that the actual hard copy of the work order be validated to facilitate inspection procedures throughout the manufacturing process.

Material Purchase
Issue Mat'l P. O.

(20) Purchasing—Upon receipt of the validated work order, the purchasing department reviews raw material inventory and issues material purchase orders as required. Material items are purchased with consideration of the scheduled manufacturing start date.

Verify
P.O./Dwg
Compliance

(21) Quality Assurance—Once a material purchase order is written, it is sent to the quality assurance department to be verified with the work order prior to being released to the supplier. This double check insures that the correct material is being purchased, thereby avoiding costly and time-consuming mistakes.

Raw Material

(22) Supplier—The material purchase order is sent to the supplier. The supplier ships the required material as specified on the purchase order.

Receive Material

(23) Material Warehouse—Material is received into the materials warehouse and stored. The material is tagged with the purchase order number it was purchased on.

Inspect Material

(24) Quality Assurance—Material is inspected for compliance with the purchase order. Any eddy current or hardness tests are performed as required. Material certifications from the supplier are checked and routed to the purchasing department.

Material Allocation

(25) Purchasing—Material is allocated to the work order.

Mfg Work Order

(26) Production Control—Once material is available and allocated, and the scheduled start date has arrived, the work order is released for manufacturing.

Issue Material

(27) Material Warehouse—Material is issued to the shop floor for manufacture.

Shop Floor Control AQS

(28) Shop Floor Control/AQS—After issue of materials, tools, and necessary tooling, the shop manufactures the parts as specified in the work order operations. Any Advanced Quality Systems (AQS) methods and techniques incorporated into the work order are maintained by the shop floor personnel.

Special Tools Tooling

(29) Shop Floor/Supervision—Any special tools and tooling that have been purchased or manufactured are routed to the appropriate operation.

CNC Program

(30) CNC Programming—Any required CNC programs are made available to the shop personnel.

Tools
Supplies

(31) Supplier—Shop personnel order and receive necessary tools and supplies to manufacture the required parts.

In-Process
Inspection

(32) Quality Assurance—Quality Assurance personnel provide any required in-process dimensional inspections, such as first articles or setup inspections.

P.O.
Outside Processing

(33) Purchasing/Outside Processing—In-process outside processes are unique operations performed by a vendor. These out-shop processes are typically machining operations that you do not have the capability of doing, or your schedule requires you to off-load.

Outside
Processing

(34) Supplier/Vendor—Operations are performed as specified on your purchase order.

Inspect
Outside Processing

(35) Quality Assurance—Outside processes and machining operations are inspected for quality and completeness.

Shop Floor
Control

(36) Shop Floor/Supervision—Work order operations are resumed, following the completion of any outside processing.

Stores
INCOMPLETE

(37) FGI/Stores—In the event a work order is stopped for any reason, the parts may be sent to a storage area until the work order is reactivated. It is common to stop work on work orders where the customer has altered the delivery schedule and the delay is sufficient enough to warrant the stoppage. Another example of why a work order may be stopped is if the work order is split after the completion of the machining operations prior to surface finishing.

Mfg
Work Order

(38) Production Control—In the event a work order is stopped for any reason, for any length of time, production control is notified.

Labor Hours
Tools/Tooling

(39) Engineering—Operational data, such as actual labor hours used to manufacture the parts, tools and tooling expenses, are sent to the engineering department to update the time standards, if necessary. This is an important step for accountability of labor hours estimated to labor hours spent. This information is vital in the improvement of the estimating and scheduling procedures.

Final Machining
Inspection

(40) Quality Assurance—Upon completion of all machining operations, quality assurance performs a final machining inspection to verify compliance with all drawing and customer purchase order requirements.

FGI Complete

(41) FGI—Parts that are complete and do not require any further processing are sent to the finished goods inventory to be logged in as complete.

P.O.
Outside Processing

(42) Purchasing/Outside Processing—A purchase order is written to procure any post machining or outside processing as shown on the manufacturing work order.

Outside Processing

(43) Vendor—Outside processing, such as surface finishing, is performed in accordance with the specifications identified on the purchase order.

Inspect
Outside Processing

(44) Quality Assurance—Outside processing is inspected for quality and completeness.

Part Mark

(45) Part Marking—Parts are marked or identified as required by customer documents and the manufacturing work order.

Inspect
Part Mark

(46) Quality Assurance—Part identification is inspected for compliance with customer requirements and accuracy.

FGI Complete

(47) FGI—Parts are received into finished goods inventory and stored as required.

Mfg
Work Order

(48) Production Control—Production control is notified of work order completion.

Issue
Pack Slip

(49) Sales—After notification of parts availability for shipment, and the scheduled ship date has arrived, the salesman issues a pack slip authorizing shipment of the parts to the customer.

Package Slip

(50) Shipping—Upon receipt of the pack slip from the sales department, the parts are pulled from FGI, packaged, and shipped to the customer.

Accounts
Receivable
Invoice

(51) Accounting—Upon receipt of a copy of the pack slip, the accounting department invoices the customer.

Receiving
Inspection

(52) Customer—The customer receives and inspects the parts for compliance with drawing documents and purchase order requirements.

Accounts
Payable

(53) Customer—The customer's accounts payable department receives notice that the parts have been received and that they comply with drawing document and purchase order requirements.

Accounts
Payable

(54) Customer—The customer's accounts payable department receives the invoice.

$$$$$

(55) Accounting—The accounting department receives payment from the customer and deposits the money in the appropriate account.

Top Shops Operations Flow Chart Description

Solicit Sales

Customer Account Manager (CAM)—Your CAM solicits sales from existing and new customers.

Issue Request For Quote

(1) Customer—The customer issues a Request For Quote (RFQ) to the salesperson. This document is typically accompanied by drawings and other specifications.

Log RFQ

(2) CAM—The RFQ is logged into the system to track the quote and assure that the quote is submitted back to the customer on time. A check is made in finished goods inventory (FGI) to note if the part has been manufactured in the past.

Identify Material Processing Tools/Tooling Operations Labor Hrs

(3) Qualified Manufacturing Team (QMT)—Upon receipt of the RFQ from the CAM, the QMT assigned to the job identifies all material requirements, any outside processing needed, tools and tooling, operation requirements, and labor or machine hours associated with those requirements.

Responsibility/Accountability—By separating the hours from the dollars within the quoting process, each team involved can then monitor and improve their estimating procedures. Once an order has been received, entered into the system, planned, scheduled, and run, the actual labor hours required to run the job and the tools or tooling expenses can then be compared to the estimate. This greatly increases the accuracy of future estimates and fine-tunes your job scheduling methods.

+Material $ Availability +Processing $ Supplier/Sched

(4) CAM—Upon receipt of the RFQ from the QMT, the CAM obtains quotes from suppliers for all material and outside processing, tools and tooling, and special requirements as identified by the QMT. Material availability is also checked and noted on the RFQ.

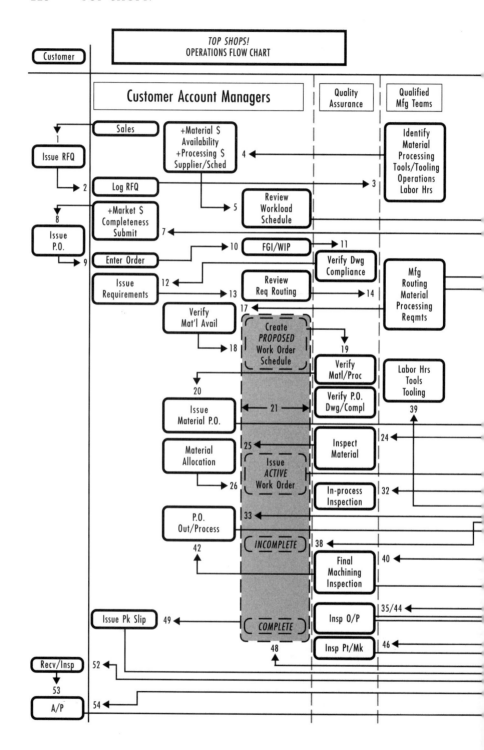

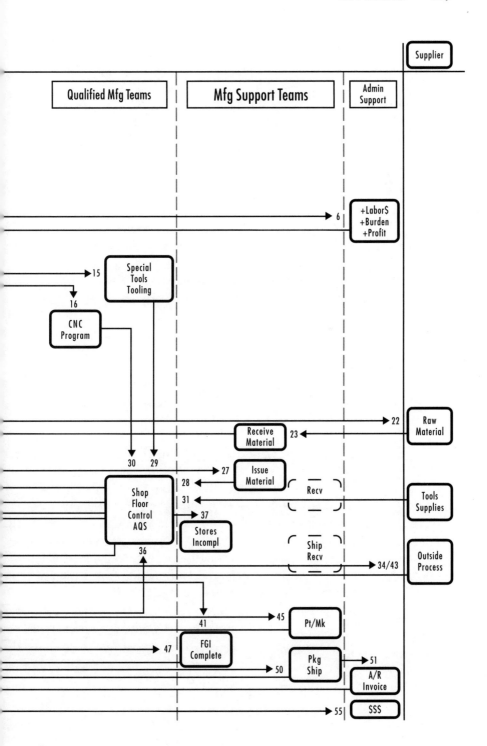

Responsibility/Accountability—Obtain the lowest price possible from the supplier. High prices only make your quote higher, thereby resulting in lost work. It is important that the person who actually buys the material from a supplier is the same person who obtains the quote! If the person who solicits quotes is not the actual buyer, the supplier is likely to quote a higher price. He would quote a more accurate price if the person soliciting the quote is the actual buyer.

Review
Workload Schedule

(5) CAM—The CAM next reviews the estimated labor and machine hours, the estimated material, and processing lead times and notes on the RFQ any scheduling considerations that may be relevant to the customer's requested delivery schedule.

Responsibility/Accountability—Maintaining an accurate production schedule is the heart of a good manufacturing operation. Promising the customer delivery dates that are unreal or not obtainable just to get the work will only anger the customer and result in a decrease of work.

+Labor $
+Burden
+Profit

(6) Accounting—The accounting department adds dollar amounts to the RFQ based on work centers used and the estimated labor hours. Work center and labor rates are developed by unique formulas designed to reveal *actual* costs incurred in manufacturing. A burden is added to the RFQ to cover all overhead expenses, and profit is added separately, only once. It is common for shops to add a percentage or dollar increase to individual items, such as material and outside processing. For example, some shops have a policy where they charge material to the customer at their cost plus 20%.

This may confuse your quoting process. It's very important to develop and list *actual* costs on your quote form. In this way the salesman knows what it's actually going to cost the company to manufacture the parts. In conversation with the customer, he then has the opportunity to negotiate the price, which ensures that the company can still make money.

Responsibility/Accountability—The accounting department is responsible for the development of actual labor hours, burden, and profit. It is important these rates be accurate.

+Market $
Completeness
Submit

(7) CAM—The CAM adds any additional dollar amounts to the bid based on what he thinks he can get for the job. After checking the quote for completeness, he submits the quote to the customer.

Responsibility/Accountability—The CAM is responsible for giving a fair and competitive price. The CAM is answerable to the customer for the price, the quality of the product, and the agreed-upon delivery date.

Issue P.O.

(8) Customer—Once all issues are resolved, the customer issues a purchase order. The purchase order includes quantities, delivery dates, and any special instructions to the company.

Enter Order

(9) CAM—Upon receipt of the purchase order, the CAM enters all necessary data into the computer or whatever system is provided, including quantities, delivery dates, and any special instructions. Should there be any future changes to the order, the CAM is responsible for making those changes in the system.

FGI
WIP

(10) CAM—The CAM next makes a check on the status of work in process (WIP) and finished goods inventory (FGI) for the part number ordered to determine if the part has been made in the past. If so, any unsold parts are identified and sent to quality assurance.

Verify
Dwg Compl

(11) Quality Assurance—Any unsold FGI parts are routed to quality assurance to be inspected for compliance with the current order requirements, including drawing and special purchase order instructions.

Issue
Requirements

(12) CAM—Upon the completion of the FGI status check, the *total quantity of parts to be manufactured* is determined by the CAM.

Review Reqmt's
Request
Routing/Info

(13) CAM—The shipping requirements are reviewed and a current routing, complete with material and processing requirements, is requested from the QMT assigned to the job.

Mfg Routing
with Material
Process Reqmts

(14) QMT—The QMT develops an accurate and complete manufacturing routing. This includes all material and processing, as well as all operational requirements, complete with setup and run-time standards.

Special Tools
Tooling

(15) QMT—The QMT notes any special tools and tooling that will be required for the job. A tooling work order is issued for the purpose of tracking labor and materials costs of tooling built in-house.

CNC Program

(16) QMT—The QMT notes any programming requirements. Required programs are created or updated by the QMT and made ready for production.

Verify
Material Availability

(17) CAM—Material and outside processing availability are verified with the suppliers for scheduling considerations. Even though availability was noted at the time of quoting, it is a good idea to obtain an update at this time because conditions change at the suppliers.

Create
PROPOSED
Work Order

(18) CAM—Run quantities are determined and a manufacturing work order is created in the system and is identified as a stage one or *proposed* work order. A *proposed* work order is simply a work order where material on hand and other issues required to manufacture the parts have not yet been resolved. The work order contains all the necessary information pertaining to material and processing requirements, including the quantity of parts to be manufactured, a manufacturing start date, and manufacturing operations.

```
┌─────────────┐
│   Verify    │
│Material Processing│
└─────────────┘
```

(19) Quality Assurance—Upon receipt of the work order, the quality assurance department verifies that the material and processing noted on the work order are in compliance with the customer's drawings, documents, and purchase order. It is important that the actual hard copy of the work order be validated to facilitate inspection procedures throughout the manufacturing process.

```
┌─────────────┐
│  Material   │
│  Purchase   │
│Issue Mat'l P. O.│
└─────────────┘
```

(20) CAM—Upon receipt of the validated work order, the CAM reviews raw material inventory and issues material purchase orders as required. Material items are purchased with consideration of the scheduled manufacturing start date.

```
┌─────────────┐
│   Verify    │
│  P.O./Dwg   │
│ Compliance  │
└─────────────┘
```

(21) Quality Assurance—Once a material purchase order is written, it is sent to the quality assurance department to be verified with the work order prior to being released to the supplier. This double check insures that the correct material is being purchased, thereby avoiding costly and time-consuming mistakes.

```
┌─────────────┐
│    Raw      │
│  Material   │
└─────────────┘
```

(22) Supplier—The material purchase order is sent to the supplier. The supplier ships the required material as specified on the purchase order.

```
┌─────────────┐
│  Receive    │
│  Material   │
└─────────────┘
```

(23) Manufacturing Support Team (MST)—Material is received into the materials warehouse and stored. The material is tagged with the purchase order number it was purchased on.

Inspect Material

(24) Quality Assurance—Material is inspected for compliance with the purchase order. Any eddy current or hardness tests are performed as required. Material certifications from the supplier are checked and routed to the purchasing department.

Material Allocation

(25) CAM—Material is allocated to the work order.

Issue ACTIVE Work Order

(26) CAM—Once material is available and allocated, and the scheduled start date has arrived, the work order is upgraded to *active* and released for manufacturing.

Issue Material

(27) MST—Material is issued to the shop floor for manufacture.

Shop Floor Control AQS

(28) QMT—After issue of materials, tools, and necessary tooling, the QMT manufactures the parts as specified in the work order operations. Any Advanced Quality Systems (AQS) methods and techniques incorporated into the work order are maintained by the QMT.

Special Tools Tooling

(29) QMT—Any special tools and tooling that have been purchased or manufactured are routed to the appropriate operation.

CNC Program

(30) QMT—Any required CNC programs are made available to the QMT.

Tools Supplies

(31) Supplier—Shop personnel order and receive necessary tools and supplies to manufacture the required parts.

In-Process Inspection

(32) Quality Assurance—Quality Assurance personnel provide any required in-process dimensional inspections, such as first articles or setup inspections.

P.O.
Outside Processing

(33) CAM—In-process outside processes are unique operations performed by a vendor. These out-shop processes are typically machining operations that you do not have the capability of doing, or your schedule requires you to off-load.

Outside
Processing

(34) Supplier/Vendor—Operations are performed as specified on the purchase order.

Inspect
Outside Processing

(35) Quality Assurance—Outside processes and machining operations are inspected for quality and completeness.

Shop Floor
Control

(36) QMT—Work order operations are resumed, following the completion of any outside processing.

Stores
INCOMPLETE

(37) MST—In the event a work order is stopped for any reason, the parts may be sent to a storage area until the work order is reactivated. It is common to stop work on work orders where the customer has altered the delivery schedule and the delay is sufficient enough to warrant the stoppage. Another example of why a work order may be stopped is if the work order is split after the completion of the machining operations prior to surface finishing.

INCOMPLETE

(38) CAM—In the event a work order is stopped for any reason, for any length of time, the work order status is changed to *incomplete*.

Labor Hours
Tools/Tooling

(39) QMT—Operational data, such as actual labor hours used to manufacture the parts, tools and tooling expenses, are noted by the QMT and routing time standards are updated, if necessary. This is an important step for accountability of labor hours estimated to labor hours spent. This information is vital in the improvement of the estimating and scheduling procedures.

Final Machining Inspection

(40) Quality Assurance—Upon completion of all machining operations, quality assurance performs a final machining inspection to verify compliance with all drawing and customer purchase order requirements.

FGI COMPLETE

(41) MST—Parts that are complete and do not require any further processing are sent to the finished goods inventory to be logged in as complete.

P.O. Outside Processing

(42) CAM—A purchase order is written to procure any post machining or outside processing as shown on the manufacturing work order.

Outside Processing

(43) Vendor—Outside processing, such as surface finishing, is performed in accordance with the specifications identified on the purchase order.

Inspect Outside Processing

(44) Quality Assurance—Outside processing is inspected for quality and completeness.

Part Mark

(45) MST—Parts are marked or identified as required by customer documents and the manufacturing work order.

Inspect Part Mark

(46) Quality Assurance—Part identification is inspected for compliance with customer requirements and accuracy.

FGI COMPLETE

(47) MST—Parts are received into finished goods inventory and stored as required.

COMPLETE

(48) CAM—The CAM is notified of work order completion. The work order status is updated to *complete.*

Issue Pack Slip

(49) CAM—After notification of parts availability for shipment, and the scheduled ship date has arrived, the CAM issues a pack slip authorizing shipment of the parts to the customer.

(50) MST—Upon receipt of the pack slip from the sales department, the parts are pulled from FGI, packaged, and shipped to the customer.

Package Slip

(51) Accounting—Upon receipt of a copy of the pack slip, the accounting department invoices the customer.

Accounts Receivable Invoice

(52) Customer—The customer receives and inspects the parts for compliance with drawing documents and purchase order requirements.

Receiving Inspection

(53) Customer—The customer's accounts payable department receives notice that the parts have been received and that they comply with drawing document and purchase order requirements.

Accounts Payable

(54) Customer—The customer's accounts payable department receives the invoice.

Accounts Payable

(55) Accounting—The accounting department receives payment from the customer and deposits the money in the appropriate account.

$$$$$

References

Aguayo, Rafael, *Dr. Deming: The American Who Taught the Japanese about Quality*. Lyle Stuart Book, Carol Publishing Group, 1990

Burleson, Clyde W., *Effective Meetings: The Complete Guide*. John Wiley & Sons, Inc., New York, 1990

Byham, William C. with Cox, Jeff, *Zapp! The Lightning of Empowerment*. Fawcett Columbine, New York, 1988

Drucker, Peter F., *Managing in Turbulent Times*. William Heinemann Ltd., London, 1980

Frank, Milo O., *How to Run a Successful Meeting in Half the Time*. Simon & Schuster, New York, 1989

Garfield, Charles, *Second to None - How Our Smartest Companies Put People First*. Business One, 1992

Glatthorn, Allan A., and Adams, Herbert R., *Listening Your Way to Management Success*. Scott, Foresman Co., 1987

Goldratt, Eliyahu M. with Cox, Jeff, *The Goal, Second Edition*. North River Press, Inc., 1992

Levering, Robert, Moskowitz, Milton, and Katz, Michael, *The 100 Best Companies to Work for in America*. Addison Wesley, New York, 1984

McCormack, Mark H., *What They Don't Teach You at Harvard Business School*. Bantam Books, New York, 1984

Nadler, Gerald, and Hibino, Shozo, *Breakthrough Thinking: The Seven Principles of Creative Problem Solving*. Prima Publishing, California, 1994

Naisbitt, John, *Megatrends - Ten New Directions Transforming Our Lives.*Warner Books, 1982

Nelson, Bob, *1001 Ways to Reward Employees.* Workman Publishing, New York, 1994

Parker, Glenn M., *Team Players and Teamwork: The New Competitive Business Strategy.* Jossey-Bass Publishers, San Francisco, 1990

Peters, Thomas J., and Austin, Nancy, *A Passion for Excellence.* Random House, 1985

Peters, Thomas J., and Waterman Jr., Robert H., *In Search of Excellence.* Harper & Row, New York, 1982

Schonberger, Richard J., *World Class Manufacturing: The Lessons of Simplicity Applied.* Free Press, New York, 1986

Thomas, John M., and Bennis, Warren G., *Management of Change & Conflict.* Penguin Books, Ltd., Middlesex, England, 1972

Tucker, Robert B., *Managing the Future - 10 Driving Forces of Change for the '90s.* G. P. Putnam & Sons, New York, 1991

Quigley, Joseph V., *Vision: How Leaders Develop It, Share It, and Sustain It.* McGraw-Hill, New York, 1993

Van Gundy, Arthur B., *Managing Group Creativity - A Modular Approach to Problem Solving.* American Management Association, New York, 1984

Waterman, Robert H., *Adhocracy - The Power to Change: How to Make Innovation a Way of Life.* Larger Agenda Series, Whittle Direct Books, Knoxville, TN, 1990

Management Advisory Group
offers software for the machine shop.
For information, write or call:
909 N. 49 St., Seattle WA 98103, (206) 632-1080
Home page: http:\\www.link1.com
E-mail: mag@link1.com

Intersect v.2.0

Intersect v.2.0 for Windows is an operations software for the job shop. Intersect easily handles traceability requirements, scheduling changes, and short run quantities. Intersect is designed to work in commercial job shops. If you have hesitated about automating your operations, now is the time to do so. Use only the modules necessary to effectively run your shop. Add new modules as you need them.

⊃ Customer Account Management (sales, order processing, production control, scheduling, purchasing)

⊃ QMT (estimating, manufacturing, planning, shop floor control)

⊃ Manufacturing Support (raw materials inventory, finished goods inventory)

⊃ Quality Assurance

StarTrack!®
The Goal Tracking Software for the Star Performer

StarTrack! is an efficient, flexible, easy-to-use software that lets you enter and track individual or team goals. Use StarTrack! to begin your goal-setting process. StarTrack! takes you through goal-setting step-by-step, offering suggestions along the way. Exit StarTrack! any time and continue when you've thought through your next step. StarTrack! offers many print options that let you view your selections. You can change or edit your entries until StarTrack! reflects exactly what you must do to succeed.

Use StarTrack! to:
☆ Identify and enter critical relationships
☆ Identify success areas
☆ Create and maintain Expectation Chart
☆ Set individual and participative goals
☆ Create intuitive and statistical goals
☆ Enter goal detail
☆ Confirm your minimum, satisfactory, and outstanding goal levels
☆ Apply the Five Goal Tests: Mission, Balance, Uniqueness, Push-Down, and 80%
☆ Print your scorecard
☆ Print charts
☆ Add trend lines
☆ Adapt individual goals to team goals, or maintain them separately
☆ Enter names of team members and define your QMTs
☆ Print the Six Point Agenda for team goals

Besides these features, use StarTrack! to analyze individual or team progress toward success. Easy entry for daily or weekly data.
Available from Management Advisory Group